T0090707

DRIFTING TOWARD LOVE

DRIFTING TOWARD LOVE

Black, Brown, Gay,
and Coming of Age
on the Streets of New York

KAI WRIGHT
Beacon Press · Boston

Beacon Press
25 Beacon Street
Boston, Massachusetts 02108-2892
www.beacon.org

Beacon Press books
are published under the auspices of
the Unitarian Universalist Association of Congregations.

11 10 09 08   8 7 6 5 4 3 2 1

This book is printed on acid-free paper that meets the uncoated paper
ANSI/NISO specifications for permanence as revised in 1992.

Text design and composition by Yvonne Tsang
at Wilsted and Taylor Publishing Services

Library of Congress Cataloging-in-Publication Data

Wright, Kai.
  Drifting toward love: black, brown, gay, and coming of age on the streets of
New York / Kai Wright.
    p. cm.
  ISBN 978-0-8070-7969-0
  1. African American gays—New York (State)—New York Metropolitan Area—
Social conditions. 2. Hispanic American gays—New York (State)—New York
Metropolitan Area—Social conditions. 3. Gay youth—New York (State)—
New York Metropolitan Area—Social conditions. 4. New York Metropolitan
Area (New York)—Social conditions. I. Title.

  HQ76.27.A37W75 2007
  306.76′60890097471—dc22   2007015759

AUTHOR'S NOTE

When I met Ryan, I was visiting family in Indianapolis—a terribly cautious and straitlaced Midwestern town—and had retreated to the coffee shop to get some work done. Procrastinating, I logged in to a gay chat room. Ryan, a twenty-two-year-old college student from Kentucky, was among the more goal-oriented guys online that evening. He messaged me.

>>Hey.
>>What's up man?
>>Not much. Where are you?

I told him. We exchanged a few pictures, bandied some small talk, and he cut to the chase: He absolutely needed to get laid.

Maybe I was drawn by the bald genuineness of his longing. Maybe I was lashing out because, even at thirty-one years old, being back in my hometown still felt stifling to my own sexuality. Or maybe I was stressed. Or restless. Or just lonely. Whatever the reason, Ryan's lust stirred my own. And I not only indulged it, I did something I knew I had no business doing: Knowing little more than each other's first names and having been acquainted for less than an hour, we had sex without a condom. We talked about it only afterward, when the conversation was long moot. We both knew we'd broken the golden rule of twenty-first-century gay life: Thou shalt not take sexual risks. It's stupid. It's a death wish.

We couldn't blame our disregard for these dictums on drugs or being in the closet or even ignorance about the risks involved, because we both knew the stakes all too well—a resurgent HIV epidemic, rising syphilis rates, a new drug-resistant strain of chlamydia. The list of perils found in uniquely high rates among young gay men is long and ever growing, and the most efficient way to transmit all of them is through unprotected anal sex. Still, there we were, having taken what seemed an incredibly dumb chance for the inescapably thin payoff of a casual hookup. "Yeah, I know," Ryan sighed as we took turns recounting the horrors of our sin. "This was bad." Then, after a pause, "Well, not *this*," he said, awkwardly waving his hand back and forth between us, "but, you know..."

Maybe not. Ryan's pronoun mix-up begged larger questions: What gamble had we each thought ourselves to be making when we lunged forward unprotected? Were we merely craving a taboo encounter, or was Ryan's stumbling effort to articulate what we had done a window into deeper needs? Perhaps we'd been groping for an equally taboo moment of vulnerability and intimacy, no matter how fleeting and misplaced. If so, did that change the risk calculation we each made?

Who knows? Certainly not me. Risk is a maddeningly slippery concept to pin down. Its relativity is boundless. Most evidently, we all measure risk differently, according to our individual needs, skills, and temperaments. A colleague of mine flies planes to relax and unwind; to my nervous mind, just boarding a commercial jet is a reckless if necessary gamble. But each of our internal demarcations of safety and danger are in constant motion as well. If I actually knew something about the mechanics of flight, for instance, I might find the whole process less daring. Knowledge changes things.

And that's how most people understand risk, as a rational choice based on the information available, however limited it may be. But emotions change things, too, in ways that aren't always rational yet are nonetheless terribly compelling—often far more so than the facts we like to believe guide our choices. In ten years of writing about the public health sector's attempt to have an impact on sexual risk-taking, it's this emotional side of the equation that I've found too often gets ignored. Particularly as it relates to gay men, we talk about risk-taking as though it occurs in a vacuum. We uproot choices like Ryan's and mine and examine them as disembodied acts of lunacy. We ask why two well-educated, conscientious young men with everything to lose would so carelessly put their health in danger for something as small as casual sex. Unable to make sense of it, we consider it pathology. As the legendary AIDS activist Larry Kramer railed in a well-received 2004 speech about the risks his younger gay brethren take, "Are you out of your fucking minds? You kids want to die."

Quite the opposite. In exploring the risks young gay men take, I've found no impulse so prominent as the urge to *live*. But time and again, in both my personal experiences and my journalism on the topic, I bump up against a fundamental challenge to that effort: the absence of space in which to build a life that incorporates all of who we are.

Even as American culture professes a steady opening to the lives of gay and lesbian people (though decidedly not transgender or bisexual ones), we are granted entrance into public life on narrowly defined terms. To the degree that we are traditionally coupled off or safely sexless, our presence is increasingly tolerated; to be simultaneously single and sexual is a far less appropriate thing. From schools to popular media to even most gay community organizing, gay sexuality itself is rarely discussed outside of the confines of the diseases it can breed. Its associated risks increasingly define it.

And for all the talk about acceptance of gay and lesbian people, too many of us look in vain for this warm embrace in our own lives and in our own communities' politics. In 2007, twenty-six states had constitutional amendments banning gay marriage. Federal law offered no protection against being fired or denied housing based on sexual orientation. Schoolyard bullies, gay-bashing thugs, and hate-spewing politicians and preachers proceeded with impunity week in and week out at all levels of society. Any effort to bridge the gap between these realities we face and the comfortably plural society America asserts itself to be is crazy-making.

Meanwhile, the frustrations of finding genuine space to exist in are compounded for gay people of color, who also struggle to fend off the false competition between racial and sexual belonging. I have written elsewhere about my own difficulties with this externally imposed dichotomy on my internal life. I delayed even self-acknowledgment of the clear emotional and sexual feelings I had for other men well into college, thickly asserting that my failure to connect with girls had little to do with my odd obsession with boys' torsos. One and one simply did not equal two, partly because there was no such number in my range of answers: I understood gay people to be white people. I knew of plenty of black faggots and punks. But gay people—people with a proud, self-proclaimed sexual identity—those were white folks who had little to do with what I knew about myself.

Young gay men must push and shove their way past these and other obstacles to their full existence, and do so with little guidance. In the best of circumstances—when not fighting against active, brutal homophobia—this is a daunting and isolating task. The education system is uselessly silent. Even parents and siblings who want to be supportive rarely have the experiences and skills to do so. Gay mentors are nearly nonexistent. And as a result, our journeys through the booby traps and pitfalls of youth can be perilous—you can get terribly lost before you discover a healthy understanding of yourself, what you want, and what you're prepared to risk to get it.

This is the broader context that I've found so often lacking as I've reported on the well-meaning and essential work of public health experts, social services providers, and gay community organizers and advocates. Indeed, this larger story just as often gets buried in my own efforts to parse the details of week-to-week happenings in the politics of sex and race. As writers and reporters, our quick-hit news stories and rapid-response analyses rarely allow time and space to attempt a genuine, holistic look at the actual lives the grand ideas and events we're covering impact. *Drifting Toward Love* is my effort to step back and consider context.

This book explores the lives of a handful of young gay men of color; some are adolescents when their story begins, others are in their early twenties. Most of the people in the book have been involved in a dispute that has gained at least local media attention in New York City: a bitter fight over the use of public space in Greenwich Village, which has pitted white homeowners against the primarily black and brown gay youth who dominate the iconic Christopher Street area. But this book does not seek to chronicle that fight or the remarkable youth political movement it spawned. Given the book's paucity of transgender and lesbian characters, it would serve as a pitifully thin retelling of that important history. Instead, I narrowly focus on the experiences of three young men, along with their friends and loved ones, and closely follow their efforts to carve out both physical and emotional space for an honest, free existence.

While none of the characters would use loaded words like "poor" or "low-income" to describe themselves, they all nonetheless live within worlds where resources are few. For each of them, the line between housed and homeless, hungry and fed, embraced and utterly alone is a thin one. For those with greater resources, like myself, the tricky challenges of jockeying for space to grow up gay are surmountable, missteps can be righted; for the young men in this book, miscalculations carry a greater price, mistakes cascade one onto the next until the notions of safety and danger lose meaning altogether.

I have focused the book's narrative on men for largely practical reasons. Reporting the story required identifying people who would not only be willing to discuss with me sensitive and difficult details of their private lives, but who would connect with me and trust me enough to sustain those conversations over several months' time. This proved challenging. The very story I sought to report repeatedly got in the way of completing it. Life's chaos overtook one person after another, and I'd lose contact with an individual as he or she fell into homelessness or the criminal justice system or simply disappeared altogether. Ultimately, the three young men profiled here are people who connected with me as another gay man of color, and who were linked to me through a shared social relation of one sort or another. There remains much to be written about the related but distinct experiences of lesbian- and transgender-identified young people.

All characters have either been given fake names or had their last names withheld, and some identifying locations and details in their stories have been changed. It's important to note that this was my choice rather than theirs. They were each prepared to stand up publicly and discuss deeply vulnerable and often unflattering details of their lives, including admitting to crimes. But identifying the main characters would necessarily identify others in their lives who have not made the same choice. I also must note that I did not witness most of the stories recounted here; they are reconstructed through dozens of hours of interviews with both the primary participants and, where possible, others who were present. I have independently confirmed those details that lend themselves to fact checking. However, in Manny's story in particular, there are events recounted here that stand largely on the protagonist's own retelling.

Above all, what struck me in reporting this book were the recurring acts of casual bravery. In the lives of the people whom I interviewed, otherwise banal events consistently turn harrowing. Yes, the circumstances they face often grow out of their own ill-considered choices. But those choices are too often forced upon them, too often consist of options that range from only bad to worse. And yet, the young people I met in reporting this book insistently push forward in their efforts to build a life in which they feel free to be who they know they are. No matter how long the odds, they persist in the belief that such a life is attainable, if they can just find the hustle that will allow them to claim it. To me, that's the choice that matters most, and it is nothing less than heroic. Of course, as one advocate working on gay youth issues replied when I said as much, "You shouldn't have to be a hero to make it through adolescence."

ONE

Just be cool, Manny's telling himself. Play it cool. At fourteen, he probably looks more shell-shocked than nonchalant, sitting here in the dead of night. But who cares? The guys stalking the Prospect Park benches understand it's all just a front anyway, that Manny's studied distraction is meant to say just the opposite about him: he's open, and ready to be approached. Manny gets this, too, or at least he does now. He's wiser than he was just a few weeks ago, aged immeasurably since that night Jason first brought him to this bizarre place. And Jason has changed an awful lot recently, too. Manny is doing his best to keep up.

The two boys had been palling around their central Brooklyn neighborhood for years before Manny's adolescent fantasies finally burst into reality. Jason lived in the same building, down on the first floor, and they'd bonded early on. Jason was tall, dark-skinned, and being a couple years older, seemed wise and seasoned to Manny. But Manny was bold for his age and thought himself to know a thing or two as well. So at around age twelve he made the first move. It was during one of their many sleepovers, and the boys were arranged side by side on the plush carpet of Jason's living room. Manny waited until they'd been lying there for long enough to have plausibly fallen asleep, then stretched out his hand and allowed it to haphazardly land in Jason's crotch. Jason neither protested nor acknowledged the maneuver, and Manny grew more brazen as a result. Their slow flirtations built and matured with age, and within a couple of years the boys were having full-on sex. They never used words like *dating* or *boyfriend,* but Manny didn't need those petty semantics anyway. This was love, plain and true.

One night not long after their affair had solidified, in the spring of Manny's ninth-grade year, they were doing their usual —lying around Jason's apartment playing video games—when Jason brought it up the first time. "Yo, let's go to the park." It was midnight.

"At *night?*" Manny had asked.

It was a strange idea. He had lived by the park since he was ten years old, and he'd never thought to go in the middle of the night. But love knows no bounds, shoves out all doubt, so Manny played it cool then too. The boys shuffled out of their building and onto the wide expanse of Eastern Parkway, a four-lane boulevard that serves as one of Brooklyn's main thoroughfares. Tree-lined esplanades frame the east- and westbound lanes, a well-placed touch of urban planning that quiets the street's hubbub and separates its workaday residential life from the incessant race of cars and trucks and gypsy cabs ferrying in and out of the borough. One side of the street is lined with squat, brick apartment buildings crammed side by side, with their block-deep warrens of rental units stretching back into the working-class neighborhood that the parkway borders. A couple of the buildings are stately and evoke the Manhattan blueblood lifestyle that developers have long hoped to recast this area of Brooklyn in the image of; others are nothing more than boxy human warehouses for the Caribbean and African American families that have long dominated the neighborhood. Manny and Jason live in one of the midrange complexes, with enough fancy casting on the facade to make it feel more upscale than it is, and from their front door they can look westward and see some of Brooklyn's most celebrated cultural landmarks along the parkway's opposite street-side. So as they walked toward the park, they passed the magnificent Brooklyn Museum—one of the nation's oldest and largest art museums, then in mid-facelift to modernize its towering, white marble facade. They strolled by the entrance to the century-old, fifty-two-acre Brooklyn Botanical Gardens and by the central branch of the Brooklyn Public Library, in its curvaceous modern-art building. And at the parkway's far western end, just a few blocks from Manny and Jason's front door, they arrived at the giant triumphant arch of Grand Army Plaza, marking the entrance to Prospect Park.

That's the passageway most park visitors stream through during the day, but Jason led Manny past it—further confusing him about their adventure. They instead veered down Flatbush Avenue, another of Brooklyn's busiest roads, which intersects Eastern Parkway as its north–south sister. Flatbush starts at the borough's iconic bridge into lower Manhattan and plunges on a southeastern diagonal into its poorer and blacker sections. For those who live to its west, Flatbush has long stood as the line of demarcation for territory into which those with means aren't supposed to venture. Things have been changing as gentrification has slowly spread eastward, but the farther south down Flatbush you travel the more that old truth still holds. And that's the direction Jason led the boys, on a fifteen-minute walk down to Prospect Park's darker, less-than-welcoming southeastern entrance.

Once inside the park, the boys wended their way up the path into a wooded area that by day hosted bird-watchers and urban hikers exploring the six-hundred-acre park's many nooks and crannies. At night, it turned into a tiny wonderland: a lively if cautious party of black and brown young men in which gender was effortlessly inverted; where normally out-of-place affectations were flaunted and young men considered grotesquely queer elsewhere became standards of beauty. The space demanded a modicum of discretion, of course, to avoid the attention of police and neighbors, but these woods had been known as gay cruising grounds for long enough that they'd been grudgingly ceded to this scene after dark.

Jason toured Manny around, greeting regulars and introducing his young beau. He was open, expansive, clearly in his element—a fact that confused Manny still further, since the two had been inseparable for months and, he thought, had shared everything about their lives. Jason knew lots of the guys, but he was particularly friendly with the young black ones; they lingered, seemed less urgent than the white men, who alighted only briefly before slipping away again.

Manny had long explored this park, but he had never imagined it hid this mysterious milieu. Still, he fancied himself worldly and experienced, so he tried hard not to show his wide-eyed amazement. He sat down with one of the regulars Jason had introduced him to, and as the two chatted they did some lines of coke. This, he figured, would settle his nerves, give him a chance to take it all in. But just as Manny was beginning to acclimate himself, he looked up to see Jason's tall, dark frame walk off into the woods with some white guy he'd been talking to.

"What the fuck?" Manny shouted. The guy he'd been snorting lines with burst into an all too knowing laughter.

Manny wasn't sure if it was the betrayal itself or Jason's casual attitude about it upon returning that so enraged him. Either way, he spurred the rage onward, let it gallop through his blood on the back of the speeding cocaine. "How can you just go off with this guy? Tell me what you did!"

Jason tried calming him.

"I got it. I *got* it," he pleaded, intending to reassure but only further confusing the situation and thereby fueling Manny's rise toward hysteria.

"I don't know what you're talking about! You think you can just go off with any nigga?"

With that, Manny knew he was crossing an unmarked but

nonetheless clear boundary, that he was declaring ownership of something he had never been given to possess. But love had wounded him, and he hadn't figured out how to stay cool in the face of that particular sort of crisis.

Finally, Jason cut to the chase and flashed $200 in Manny's face. "Sometimes I have a part-time job," he began, pausing to let the idea sink into his young lover's head, then laying it plain when it became clear Manny wasn't going to sort it out on his own. "Sucking dick is what I do best, so I might as well put it to use."

And so here they are again, back in the park three weeks later, Manny determined to show Jason and himself that he, too, has useful skills. All he has to do is be cool, let the buyers take the lead. After all, he and Jason have the market cornered. He's easily the youngest hustler here, so they'll bag anybody with a fetish for little black boys. And this is a place for fetishes, to be sure, a place to fill the empty vessels of unknown faces and disembodied sex organs with quietly held dreams and desires.

Manny's not sitting at the chess tables long before Jason steers somebody his way. The man is prototypical of the tricks Manny will come to know in this park: a short, nondescript white guy, maybe in his thirties, maybe his forties—they're all pretty old, to his teen eyes anyway, and it's always dark. Manny follows the man down a path leading away from the main clearing until they find a spot that provides just enough privacy. The guy stops and leans against a tree.

"Can you take off your pants," he stage-whispers, his voice low and heavy.

Manny obliges, drops his trousers around his ankles and waits for further instructions. The man unzips his jeans and starts massaging his penis. He's wearing a loud plaid shirt, and Manny hates it, thinks it a particularly awful outfit.

"Can you turn around," the man asks, tempering his direction as a polite request.

Manny again takes his cues, and as he's rounding through

his third, slow twirl he notices the man's head is reared back, that he's not even paying attention to the awkward dance he's requested. Manny watches the man moan and shake through the climax of whatever fantasy his lithe body has facilitated, and as he does so he quietly slips into his own reverie. This, he thinks, is easy money.

A couple of hours later, Jason and Manny sit on the park benches pooling the night's take. It's after two in the morning by now, and the park's furtive buzz has died down. They've pulled down a few hundred dollars between them, mostly owing to Jason's ability to make quick work of his tricks. Manny turned just three guys, himself. They weren't all as easy as the first; he even had to give one of them a blow job. But for a fourteen-year-old on the fast road from recreational to habitual coke use, this kind of hourly wage can't be easily dismissed. Plus, he and Jason will do this together, as an unstoppable team. So they resolve to come twice a week, consciously picking the days on which Manny doesn't have to be at school until later than usual the following morning. He's making it to school less and less often these days, but he's still enrolled and feels some need to respect that fact in idea if not in deed.

Not that Manny is one of *those* kids, one of the lost-from-the-start, nihilist children of the '90s caricatured in the era's popular media. As he sat plotting a career in sex work, Manny actually still had a good bit going for him, in all the obvious ways at least—access to a relatively good education; a ferociously dedicated mother; a wide network of engaged adults. And even as he'd spend the coming summer flailing about Prospect Park— selling his mouth, his ass, his youth, his mocha-brown skin— in a parallel world he'd remain the sort of boy adults deem to have "potential." That was the irony of Manny's rebellious posture. He managed a disaffection that steered around teen angst and arrived instead at precocious. And Manny was indeed a capable kid, which is why he was more certain than anyone of his own ability to chart a course through life. But he'd already come to the conclusion that there was no preexisting map out there for people like him. No, Manny knew even at fourteen that if he was going to make it to the other side of the rainbow, he'd have to find the way on his own. And in the spring of 2000, the road to Manny's happiness led through Prospect Park's eastern gates.

Prospect Park's history of place is long. The land was first developed by African slaves who built the homesteads of early European settlers, establishing Brooklyn as a sleepy agrarian outpost. In the early 1800s, the area's development hastened as New Yorkers sought a suburban retreat from Manhattan's increasingly dense and frenetic life, turning Brooklyn into the country's third largest city by the 1860s. Civic leaders quickly realized a need to offer their growing masses a respite inside Brooklyn, and in 1866 Central Park's famed design team of Calvert Vaux and Frederick Law Olmsted answered the call with an ambitious plan for a sprawling nature reserve, including thick woods filled with exotic flora from around the world. Olmsted believed strongly that urban areas needed internal retreats so that all classes of people could escape the city's chaos and miasma, not just those with the resources to live on the rural outskirts; Prospect Park, like Central Park, was to be a place where poor and working-class folks could get away from it all and heal themselves. Manny and the men he cruised the park's woods with felt they were doing just that—even if it wasn't exactly what Olmsted had in mind.

But that's urban America. New York is a place where scarce space is jealously defined by whomever has most recently laid claim to it. Places bear names loaded with meaning—Harlem is steeped in the history of black arts and intelligentsia; Bensonhurst evokes rough-and-tumble Italian American neighborhoods; the Upper East Side oozes with old wealth; and the West Side from Greenwich Village through Chelsea explodes with gay pride. From Little Italy to Little Odessa, New Yorkers stake out their space and draw power and belonging from it. But here, in what is arguably the gay cultural capital of the world, adolescents who don't fit into heterosexual norms and grow up in neighborhoods like Manny's—working-class, largely black and Latino—look in vain for their own place to call home. Pride rallies rarely march down their blocks, and certainly don't linger when they do; the adult, largely transplanted, and almost entirely white and well-heeled world of gay Manhattan offers them no warmer welcome. And so, central Brooklyn's young black and Latino gay men mark Vaux and Olmsted's rambling woods as theirs—a place to hang out, meet friends and lovers, and, sure, maybe also pick up a few bucks from the older guys who drop in for a visit.

The young people who inhabit these sorts of spatial margins preoccupy the minds of social scientists. They are among the most worrisome in that social category that has come to be known as "at risk"—for Manny, Jason, and thousands of young people like them are indeed at the top of the list for a disturbing array of today's worst ills. Homeless-services providers have long estimated that gay, lesbian, bisexual, and transgender youth account for anywhere from 20 to 40 percent of young people without homes. One study found that more than a quarter of gay youth surveyed had dropped out of school, citing harassment as a leading reason. Another study found a third of gay high school kids had attempted suicide in the previous year. Still more have found gay youth more likely to use drugs, alcohol, and tobacco. And among all of this bad news, HIV/AIDS looms largest, particularly for young black men. In the mid-1990s the Centers for Disease Control and Prevention found HIV infection rates among fifteen- to twenty-two-year-old black gay and bisexual men to be as high as 14 percent—a number on par with the worst epidemics globally, and twice that of their white counterparts. In 2005 the CDC reported that new HIV infections among twenty- to twenty-four-year-old gay men of all races spiked a whopping 47 percent between 1999 and 2003; 60 percent of those infected were black.

So the question must be asked: What drives all this risk? Certainly Manny and his cohort have made a series of choices that leave them vulnerable to physical dangers. But what contexts are those choices made within? Risk is, after all, an entirely relative concept. And the physical vagrancy of Brooklyn's gay kids is indicative of a larger emotional reality: they are cultural refugees, wandering in search of an identity and a belonging. For some it begins in early childhood, for others not until adolescence, but the gap between themselves and the worlds they navigate too often defines them—and it is in that divide where the question of risk must be examined.

For the last several months of eighth grade, Manny had a ritual. He'd get up first thing in the morning and head out for a long, full day. He'd trudge down to the subway and ride the train up to East Fifty-seventh Street. His school was near his apartment in Brooklyn, of course, but he had lost interest in that; his mind was in Trump Tower. Manny wasn't drawn by the building's iconic wealth and power. Nor did he care to explore the legion of tony shops that stretch from its gilded entrance down Fifth Avenue. No, the main attraction was Michael, the doorman at the Tower's residential building. Manny remembers Michael as more of a diversion than a person, "just a cool black guy" who made him laugh with boastful stories about Coney Island, the worn-down beach neighborhood that he hailed from and considered to be a little piece of paradise in Brooklyn. He loved that Michael gave him cigarettes, as he couldn't yet pull off buying them himself, but most of all he liked that Michael let him hang around and kill time without bugging him too much about being a truant. The pair would smoke cigarettes and talk about nothing for a couple of hours, then Manny would go around the corner to the Trump Tower's Fifth Avenue shopping mall entrance. "I'd go in there, have breakfast at this cafeteria, in this sort of dining area," Manny recalls. "Then I'd go in the Tower Records and just like listen to records, for like three hours. I don't know why they didn't call the police on me. I was there every day, and I never bought a record there. Ever."

Music was important to Manny, and to his then-burgeoning relationship with Jason. Despite the couple years' difference in their ages, Manny and Jason had started hanging out, since most kids in their building were either much older or much younger than both of them. Jason's dad traveled a lot, and his mom worked nights. That gave Jason a lot of time alone, allowed him to live out hours of each day however he pleased. And Manny admired that sort of freedom, longed to have it himself. For the time being, he approximated independence by attaching himself to Jason's.

But it was Jason's passion for music that first drew Manny's attention and offered the boys an initial common ground. Whatever Jason's persona out on the street, Manny recognized something in him when it was just the two of them, and it came out particularly with music. Manny exploited the shared interest to probe for more. He'd hold out his beloved divas, dangling them before Jason as canaries in the mine of sexual exploration and delighting when Jason shared his enthusiasm. "We were into the same things, kinda faggoty in the same way behind closed doors," Manny explains. "I remember some Céline Dion thing happening, and feeling like we could bond over that."

Jason's own collection stretched from 1960s folk great Otis Redding to techno artist Niko. He'd mix and match the tunes into playlists on cassette tapes, then label each according to the mood it was meant to accompany—there was "sad-love" for the sappy moments, or "shit my pants" for those fraught days that defied emotional vocabulary. The boys lay around Jason's apartment night after night, playing video games as Jason wowed Manny with his music library, and as Manny carefully shepherded their friendship into a romance.

But as much as Manny loved Jason and his music, he harbored another side that he felt few people in his life could really engage him on. He read the newspaper every day, and had been doing so for a while. He devoured books, primarily political and social histories. He couldn't get enough of politics and was eager to jump into debate over the issues with whoever could keep up. This inclination came partly by upbringing—most of the adults in his life had always been politically conscious and engaged in some way; his mom was a social worker. But it also seemed innate. Manny had leadership skills so natural he was all but unable to control them. Once, annoyed by how little time a teacher allowed to prepare for an exam—which he had no intention of studying for anyway—he rallied the whole class in boycott. Another time, he led a petition drive against the school lunch menu's unhealthy choices and marched it over to the superintendent's house himself. The political histories he pored over fueled all of this.

They also made Manny a remarkably articulate and literate eighth grader, which he says is the main reason he made it to school only about once a week during the last few months of that academic year. His grades weren't stellar, particularly in math. But he'd scored in the top percentile in reading and English on the standardized tests that help determine the future for New York's middle schoolers. Most of the city's high schools aren't zoned by neighborhood. Instead, kids pick a slate of schools they'd like to attend and then compete for entry as though they were applying for college. By winter, Manny's high test scores had assured him admittance to his first choice—a brand-new college prep program in lower Manhattan—and so he saw little point in continuing to labor over the tedium of a curriculum he considered below him. Not to mention that he'd long developed a reputation for having an attitude problem and an explosive temper.

So why bother? He figured he'd rather spend his days at Trump Tower. "There used to be this little bookshop upstairs, like antique books," Manny fondly recalls. "There was this old white man. He had like one string of hair that he would comb over—such a weirdo! And he would just let me sit there and read. So I was just reading, all day. God, there was some book that I just *had* to finish, and it was terrible. It was like akin to *Jane Eyre*, but I don't know what it was. It was bad. It was in Old English."

Once he started ninth grade, however, Manny reengaged passionately. The school was staffed with young teachers eager to feed hungry minds, and Manny's was famished. It was also stoked for combat. He'd storm into class spoiling for a fight, and usually find one. When the teacher assigned *Heart of Darkness,* he dramatically registered his outrage "as a black person in America!"

He figures most of his teachers took this edge as the intellectual eagerness it was—and that most of his classmates found it as bizarre as he found them. It was a small school of primarily privileged kids, and very few of them shared his brown skin. Feeling truly connected to no group, he flitted around, making acquaintance with all of them—he'd be just as likely to lunch with the few black girls as skulk about with the white skater kids.

His only real confidante was Lisa. With her towering six-foot frame and stout build, the brainy Jewish girl felt like just as much of a misfit as Manny, and they bonded over being intellectually combative in global studies class. "She was just really smart and sort of depressive, and that kind of got us together, feeling tragically excluded from the rest of the world," Manny observes in typically dry self-deprecation. The two mainly reinforced one another's preemptive strikes against the pack they felt left out of. Manny was well into the process of cultivating a bad apple image to augment his brainy cockiness and explain his perennially awkward fit, to himself if no one else, and Lisa indulged the performance. Their bond coincidentally positioned Lisa to eventually offer Manny singular support in his unfolding tragedy.

A couple of Manny's classmates did, however, have something he hadn't realized he was missing until he found it: a notion of what it might be like to live as a gay teen. Melissa was his entrée. She was a couple of grades ahead, but Manny had taken notice of her shaved head and the lavender triangles she stitched onto her backpack, all bold announcements of her posture as an open, unapologetic lesbian. Indeed, she went further. Melissa considered herself "queer," a moniker that signifies an identity rooted as much in political inclinations as in sexual ones. Like many politically engaged young gay people, Melissa didn't seek the tolerance offered in mainstream discourse about sexuality, and she wasn't particularly concerned with the gay movement's drive for civil equality either. Or, more precisely, those things were necessary but not nearly enough. Melissa wanted to dig up the cultural roots of sexual and gender norms and replant them as something entirely new, something that abandons norms altogether rather than tolerating or equalizing digressions from them. This was the stuff a queer sexual identity was about and it resonated with Manny. Plus, like Jason, Melissa flaunted an independence he respected; she'd already left behind a troubled relationship with her parents and moved in with a girlfriend in her early twenties. She was somebody Manny figured could show him a thing or two about life, introduce him to new worlds and possibilities. So he reached out to befriend her.

Their slow courtship culminated one day over lunch.

Manny's social promiscuity had brought him into contact

with "the popular girls," a crowd Melissa deeply distrusted, and she pulled her young charge aside to counsel him on the dangers with which he was flirting. These girls are catty and backbiting, she warned. Don't tell them all your business or you'll find it out in the street. It wasn't just teenage pettiness; this was Melissa revealing the soft, mothering side she worked hard to conceal from the world at large. The openness of her sexual identity put her out on a ledge all by herself, leaving her uniquely vulnerable. Like many young queers, she donned a hard outer shell to insulate herself from the ridicule her honesty drew, in the same way Manny and Lisa sought safe-haven in their rebellious, outsider postures. Still, Manny shrugged Melissa's warnings off as part of an intragender fight that wasn't his own. "I was like, 'Melissa, the popular girls don't like you because they think you're trying to sleep with them. They love me.' "

But all the talk about discretion nonetheless provided Manny an opportunity for candor. He hadn't been actively hiding his relationship with Jason and the world they shared back in Brooklyn; he'd just chosen not to bring it up at school—and certainly not to bring Jason around. He liked his worlds divided, separated out into boxes he could manage independently. And as he moved to open up to Melissa, he had no intention of knocking any holes in those boxes, he just wanted to add a new one. So he thanked Melissa for her advice on the perils of popularity and changed the subject to a more appealing topic.

"I want to tell you something," he offered. "I'm kind of queer."

Manny and Melissa henceforth considered the lunch his "coming out of the closet" moment, that dramatic instance of crossing the breach from straight to gay—which was an odd idea, given that Manny hadn't previously thought himself to be in the closet, or even really understood what that meant. It implied a weirdly binary world of before and after organized around his sexuality, which was something he valued, sure, but that didn't define him in the way this in- and out-of-the-closet dichotomy suggested. And while he had by now learned about shame surrounding homosexuality, he didn't think he felt any of it himself. His discretion about sharing his relationship with Jason at school had been less about their sexuality than the range of clear, uncomfortable differences his whole Brooklyn life presented; he didn't think these kids could possibly understand him, so why try opening up? But with Lisa, for instance, he had never really shielded any part of his life, Jason included. He'd always casually talked to her about whatever he and Jason were up to—though, as their exploits would grow more illicit later in the year, he'd be careful to omit anything that was too far out there. Maybe it was the political nature of their original bond, or maybe it was the outcast vibe of their friendship, but for whatever reason, he could let his guard down with Lisa, and the thought of hiding that he was homosexual from her never occurred to him.

Still, all of that had just been behavioral: he'd fallen in both love and lust with another guy, and it didn't mean much more than that. With Melissa, however, he was now trying on an *identity* to go with that behavior, and bringing to it a larger meaning that could have implications for all aspects of his life. "I didn't know what to call it," Manny explains of his sexuality prior to meeting Melissa. "But by the time I came out to her, I was like, OK, this is what I am."

It was a compelling notion, but one he'd have trouble implementing in practice. He'd set down a path with Melissa to explore and develop this sexual identity, but both the process and its outcome would remain segregated not just from his sexual and romantic life with Jason but also from everything he called home.

Melissa worked evenings at a coffee shop down by Washington Square Park, in the heart of Manhattan's Greenwich Village. She was the anchor in her social scene, and her necessarily queer friends would gather around her every day at the shop to hang out. Hoping to meet more gay teens, Manny started going there, too, and these afternoons eventually led to both his first infectious brush with activism and his initial, chafing scrape up against social services.

The real catalyst for this movement was Andy, his first close gay friend. Melissa had been the draw into queerness and its social rituals, but Andy became a reason to keep coming. The boys were peers only to the extent that Manny resculpted himself to fit into Andy's world. A lanky, white fifteen-year-old with a clear-eyed view of the gay life he wanted and a suburban rebel's affinity for coloring his hair, Andy lived outside of the city and went to private school, but he made the forty-five-minute trip down to Greenwich Village every afternoon to hang out in Melissa's coffee klatch. As far out of the way as the daily routine took him, he nevertheless traveled a much shorter emotional distance than Manny. The café sat just north of Washington Square, a block-long, concrete park that has long been a touchstone for white youth counterculture. On sunny afternoons, edgy-looking teens roll and bounce off its surfaces on their skateboards and rollerblades; they mingle uneasily but peacefully with the preppie undergrads of New York University, which dominates the middle regions of the Village and surrounds Washington Square. A guy like Andy fits right into the mix. Manny was at best a savvy tourist, devouring new sights and sounds and quickly learning to manipulate them for his immediate needs, but never quite making them his own.

Andy's primary obsession was losing his virginity, and he'd identified the stylish young men idealized in gay magazines and television shows like *Queer As Folk* and *Will and Grace* as his quarry—or, as Manny puts it, "Andy really liked white boys." By this point, Manny himself already had an active sex life with Jason, but he played his sexual maturity as happenstance for Andy, leaking just enough drips and drabs to keep him a com-

forting step ahead—he had his bad-boy image to think of—
without creating an unbridgeable distance between them.
They'd break off from the group in Melissa's coffee shop and
ramble through the Village's hodgepodge of streets. Heading
east takes you into the area's more gritty blocks, once known for
its radical arts scene and raging heroine trade but now more frat
party than anything else; westward are the more rarefied blocks,
lined with clothing boutiques and bag stores and cozy restaurants, many of them targeting gay yuppies or tourists or both.
That's the direction Andy and Manny would usually head, figuring they were positioning themselves inside the gay culture they
aspired to. As they walked, Andy did most of the talking. "He
was giving me more detail than I was giving him," Manny explains of the conversations, during which Andy would lay out
the plot of each date that he hoped would end with him getting
laid. "He was like, 'We're going here and then doing this.' I
might tell him, like a week after, 'Oh yeah, I had sex.' "

Together, Andy and Manny followed Melissa's lead and began participating in the Lesbian and Gay Community Center's
youth program, affirmatively crowned with the acronym YES,
for Youth Enrichment Services. YES was after-school program-
ming of sorts for lesbian, gay, bisexual, and transgender youth,
on its most basic level, simply offering them someplace where
they could come each day and just feel safe being a queer teen,
while participating in diversions ranging from art projects to
activism.

After hanging in the coffee shop and walking around the Village, Andy and Manny would wrap up their afternoon by heading over to the YES drop-in center. Manny took to it fast. The
center was putting together a conference for queer youth activists and he rolled up his sleeves to help with the planning and
promoting. He liked everything about it, from the politics to just
having something tangible to which he could tie this vague new
concept of sexual identity. At the center, being queer meant

doing things. It meant handing out flyers and participating in meetings and taking notes and rendezvousing at specific, increasingly familiar places, and just generally being part of something.

And going to the center also gave Manny a chance to breathe. While he couldn't articulate it at the time, he felt a nagging need to put some space between himself and Jason and their intensifying exploits. They wouldn't end up tricking in Prospect Park until the end of the school year, and their drug use remained largely haphazard and experimental at the year's outset, playing around with intoxicants at parties and in Jason's apartment. But already Manny felt stifled by the relationship—and by his life back on Eastern Parkway in general. Hanging out with Andy at the center didn't do anything to ease his overall discomfort inside all of the worlds he navigated, but it did offer a starkly contrasting experience from lying around playing video games with Jason and worrying about the slow but steady shifts he'd noticed in his lover's demeanor. "I think that ultimately I needed a way to talk about what was happening to me," Manny explains, sighing at the now-grating memory of the confusing juggling act his varied lives demanded. "I just needed like a second to think about it. And Jason was not about thinking." So he threw himself into Andy and Melissa and YES in hopes of finding something new, something that would at least bring all his boxes into alignment, if not make them one. "I don't think I'd come to a place where that stuff I did with Jason looked ugly yet," he says. "I wanted a better way to incorporate it into my queer identity—that was something that I was really proud of."

The connecting threads, however, would remain elusive for some time.

TWO

Like most of its residents, the little white house at the northern
end of Crystal Street is a work in progress, one of the seemingly
dozens of neighborhood projects Lionel's always juggling,
though this one is his home too. It's home to a whole lot of
people, actually, but Lionel's got a handyman streak that keeps
him fussing around the place, putting up walls here, taking
them down there, constantly shifting and morphing the internal
structure to accommodate an equally steady ebb and flow
of housemates. And the old two-story fixer-upper in Brooklyn's
East New York has definitely come a long way since he and the
other two nominal owners moved into it back in 2001. The
warm hominess of the space mitigates the swirling chaos it often hosts. The living room and kitchen are splashed with bright,
bold, defiant colors—oranges, yellows, reds—and a giant mural
depicting an underwater wonderland covers a long stretch of
wall connecting the two big open spaces; beadwork designs
of moons and seascapes cover the cabinets. The bedrooms upstairs are cramped, sure, but also cozy. The basement's been
converted into a comfortable but cluttered office, its walls lined
with books and posters bearing the slogans of social-change
movements. Rows and stacks of books, magazines, pamphlets,
and literature of all sorts are everywhere in the house, actually—
community-organizing case studies and political economies

and queer-studies tracts and black-empowerment discourses. It all adds up to make Lionel look terribly out of place in his own home, an incongruent presence in his paint-splattered dungarees and work boots, his long black hair snatched back into a bun, with the loose strands radiating out to give him a frayed, scattered look.

And today he is, as always, scattered. He's just walked up the stoop and found the front door standing wide open, the phone ringing. It's for Julius. A mutual friend's trying to find Julius to give him some much needed work, which is a welcome development in Lionel's mind, given how far back Julius is on rent and other house bills. He carries the wireless phone out onto the stoop and looks up and down Crystal, but sees no sign of him. Lionel figures he must be somewhere with Legba, the house's muscle-bound, lovable meathead of a dog. So he takes a message and strolls down Crystal in search of the duo; he doesn't want Julius to let this job opportunity pass.

Crystal's a typical East New York block. Small one- and two-story homes sit cheek by jowl along either side of the street, some with their few feet of front yard fenced off in a vague nod at suburbia, others with short, blunted stoops that dump straight out onto the sidewalk. Squat brown apartment complexes are sprinkled throughout the neighborhood, their facades spotted by window-unit air conditioners, fire escapes zigzagging up and down the front and back. Corner stores, universally known as bodegas by New Yorkers, mark most major intersections; though here their shelves are crammed only with dried goods and potato chips and snack cakes rather than fresh fruits; the fridge is stocked with tallboys of beer rather than with protein shakes. Both the homes and the apartment buildings are uneven. A line of dilapidated apartment complexes will be interrupted by a new, prefabricated-looking structure of oddly pink-tinted bricks, framed by freshly laid concrete sidewalks and steps. The houses that are occupied are tended to fastidiously, with freshly painted siding and homey flower arrangements. But a neighboring structure's windows will be boarded up with wood planks that are warping and fading in a sign of just how long they've sat in place, the remnants of a sun-bleached eviction notice still stapled to the door.

If Lionel stands out inside his house, he seems right in place once he's out on Crystal. East New York is overwhelmingly black and Latino, and Lionel is Korean. But he radiates the brand of masculinity expected of a twenty-nine-year-old man in this kind of hood. He towers at six feet two and struts along with the approachable self-assurance of someone who's got nothing to fear. He's open and friendly with everybody he sees, be they little old ladies or young drug slingers working the corner, but he also projects a strength during those interactions that puts people at ease; he knows that comfort in turn makes everybody less likely to start shit with him.

Lionel walks a block up Crystal and rounds the corner onto Gary Avenue, heading for the community garden one of the neighborhood's elders created out of twelve abandoned lots fifteen years ago. The old man had hoped the garden would be an oasis for the community. And it had been, not just for others but for the man's own sons in their younger years—all of his boys, though, were ultimately swallowed up by the neighborhood's drug businesses; they offer reliable, high-paying work, if you can stand the violence. His kids have all spent time in prison upstate, but the garden has lived on. And its upkeep is one of the projects Lionel pours his heart into; all the folks at the Crystal Street house do. It offers a spot where they can hold community yoga classes or have picnics or stage food drives or just come and read and take in the beauty.

Lionel spots Julius inside the garden and opens the tall chain-link fence that separates the concrete from the grass. Julius is sitting on a plastic toy picnic table, petting Legba and lecturing about the varying strategies for nursing fruits versus vegetables out of the garden's soil.

"This is a fruit tree. I don't know which one it is," he says, laughing at the gap between the breadth and depth of his agricultural knowledge. "It's a citrus tree, maybe lime." He turns and ticks off the rest of the garden's bounty, pointing to each as he names them—eggplants, strawberries, grapes, an apple tree. Lionel, polite even when he's clearly annoyed, excuses his interruption and then tempers his admonition with a friendly taunt.

"You left the door open, fool."

He hurriedly relays the message about the work opportunity and reminds Julius of an organizational detail for another gig they've got, hauling somebody's furniture in the house van, and then rushes back to his chores. Legba runs across the grass and leaps and paws at the far-side fence, where a gaggle of plain-clothes vice cops have stopped on the sidewalk to hang out and talk. Julius cuts his eyes and sucks his teeth at the scene before whistling and calling Legba back to our side of the garden. You never know what's gonna set those cops off and start up some mess, he explains, before returning to his gardening lesson.

Julius is one of those Lionel worries about. The twenty-two-year-old's sheer power is just unsettling. It starts with his evident beauty—the bright smile, the cherub-like innocence of his round face; his smooth, dark skin and baby dreads—all of which works alongside a sharp, speedy mind and a disarming charm to concoct a potent, volatile brew. His physicality is unquestionably male—he's nearly six feet tall, with square shoulders and rounded if unsculpted musculature that he shows off in tight shirts and tank tops. But he wields his manhood in an overtly feminine way; where Lionel struts, Julius swishes. And this recasting of male form in female style creates a gender play that's more take-no-shit diva than nelly boy. Julius is cut out for big things, and knows as much. But there's no telling exactly what the nature of his large-scale acts will be on any given day; he's equally capable of stunning achievement and devastating self-destruction.

There are so many young folks like this in Lionel's life these days. Indeed, many of them live with him. This wasn't how he and his friends pictured things turning out when they bought the house. They never saw themselves running a makeshift youth shelter, and certainly not one for queer kids like Julius, since all of the owners of the house were straight at the time they bought it. But here they are, serving as part mentor, part friend, part disciplinarian, but often just as a plain stabilizing force in the lives of what at its peak had been nearly a dozen young people crammed into the four bedrooms of their commune-style home. There was the fourteen-year-old who'd been kicked out of his house and his school; the young lesbian who'd been squatting with a dozen kids in an empty building uptown; another young woman who still technically lived with her family in this neighborhood but spent most of her time at the Crystal Street house, where she felt safer than she did on her own block. And there was Julius.

Julius's day starts around two in the afternoon, at the computer in the basement. He loves tennis, and the first stop on his cyber rounds is always the Women's Tennis Association Web site, where he checks the latest scores and doings on the circuit. He also likes to stay up on the news, so he'll usually read the New York Times and check out some international news sites. Then there're his online games of canasta and spades, which he goes at for a couple of hours.

Of course, he'll also do a few hours of work. Lionel and the others ask everybody staying in the house long-term to at least make a good faith effort to come up with $200 a month, which gets funneled into expenses for the house and its affiliated community-building projects. Julius is perennially indebted on this score, but lately he's been making good money as a "ghostwriter" for students at the technical college where his friend Miriam is studying to be a medical assistant. Julius is good at learning things, once he gets his curiosity revved up. He'd been an honor student at his high school in Florida before he ran away from his foster family down there and turned up in New York. So when he started tutoring Miriam in some of the program's basic math work, her grades shot up. She brought an exam home one day and he did it for her; copies circulated the school and a small business was born. Now he gets $50 a pop to write students' papers for them.

"I'm fucking reading these books online about urinalysis," he says, bursting into an expansive, high-pitched laugh that falls just shy enough of a squeal. He cranks out fifteen or so of the short papers a month, hitting everything from "administrative competencies" like working with spreadsheets to briefs on various diseases and conditions.

"Everyone says, 'How can you do this?'" He shrugs, sucks his teeth, and dismisses the question as absurd. "Miss honey"—that's Julius's standard windup when he's about to break something down—"President Bush did it! He didn't go to school. He was hanging and fucking somebody while somebody was doing his papers and studying for him. So, why not?"

But the irony of the whole thing's not lost on a guy as bright as Julius. The Crystal Street house is the tenth place he's called home since arriving in the city three years ago. He's stayed with boyfriends, bunked in city shelters, even made a run at teaming up with roommates in their own place, subsidized by a local housing program. None of it has proved permanent. The bottom always falls out, turning his life upside down and sending him scurrying back into the streets in search of the basics—food, shelter, good company with which to pass the hours. Could things have been different for him? What if he had gone to college instead of conning his high school guidance counselor—the one adult who ever seemed to really care about him—into helping him hop a bus up to New York City? What if he'd spent any of the time since then investing in his future rather than hanging out, smoking pot, and clubbing as he surfed the city's emergency aid programs for homeless youth?

What if he could just put all of his brain and body and plain *soul* power to work for himself? "I could go get a regular nine to five, or even a twelve to eight, I could go back and ..." He trails off into a rare moment of transparent self-doubt and melancholy. "I have so many qualifications to work in any nonprofit organization that serves people of color," he says, speaking with the jargony expertise of someone who's had recurring experience as both a client and a volunteer for those groups. "But I just haven't had the motivation to do that."

He's motivated elsewhere.

Today's youth are renowned for their electronic multitasking and Julius is no different. As he's online reading news and playing games and researching papers he also logs in to Adam4Adam, a dating site where thousands of largely black and Latino men go to cruise for sex, love, and all manner of virtual connection with other men. Dating and cruising sites targeting gay men are plentiful, often subdivided by genre, geography, and even fetish. Most of them blend an unabashed sexual ethos with the social networking typical of Web sites more familiar to popular culture, like MySpace and Friendster. Members create profiles with pictures of themselves and descriptions of their likes and dislikes, but in addition to hobbies and bands those preferences can include favored sex acts and characteristics of the guys you want to do it with. Adam4Adam is distinct in that it's a site that, over time, has become a space nearly exclusive to black and Latino gay men. Gay America is no different from the rest of the country in that it is deeply segregated on matters of love and lust, and on most gay chat sites, users regularly spell out in their profiles which races they're willing to be approached by—"sorry, only into whites and Asians"; "no blacks, just a preference"; "hung blatino guys a +++"; and so on. Such distinctions aren't necessary on Adam4Adam, because the few white guys you'll find there have already made their proclivities clear just by logging in to the site in the first place. Instead, the prohibitions broadcast in Adam4Adam's profiles are more likely to involve gender, with members of all gender expressions in seeming agreement that butch is good and faggoty is bad—"no sissies," "be a man," "real niggas only!"

The site is wildly popular. Ages range from Julius's eighteen- to twenty-two-year-old set on up to guys in their sixties. Log in at almost any hour in New York City, or in any major metropolis around the country, and you'll find hundreds of men there chatting and e-mailing back and forth. And even with all of the cut-to-the-chase sexual language, there are as many people looking for simple friendship and connection as there are horny guys looking for quick hookups. Indeed, as on all the gay chat sites, members often seem to have their wires crossed on what they want to get out of the virtual space. Members build profiles that accept and reinforce a tacit agreement that the space be reserved for meeting physical needs, but then back into pleas that it accommodate emotional desires as well. So one profile after another leads with overt sexuality—naked pictures and graphic descriptions of sexual skills—only to then wind into protestations that the person's really more than a sex act, that he needs and can give something else too: "Don't be fooled by my profile name," a typical refrain will go, "not just looking for a fuck, so come correct."

But Julius isn't one of those people, he's clear that he goes to Adam4Adam for "no-strings" sex and has built a stable of "fuck buddies" there, fifteen or so guys he turns to in the numb hours between when he gets bored with the computer and when he goes out clubbing or climbs back into bed. There's "NYCBiggestPimp," the nameless Secret Service officer who's "a weird guy, but good in bed." There's Marty, who has a couple of girlfriends—or, as Julius puts it, "baby-mama drama chics." There's Doug, who Julius is fond of but who lives sorta far away —meaning not on the subway line that intersects with Crystal Street, thus requiring either a bothersome train transfer or a

$20 cab ride. Julius's preference for guys that live near the A train or, better still, in walking distance draws up the incongruity of these trysts: they're not compelling enough to go out of the way for, yet are so essential that he has as many as three of them a week.

Julius is also careful to limit the intimacy of his sexual encounters. None of the men know where he lives or how to reach him outside of e-mail. If you're to fuck Julius, you don't call him; he calls you. And there's no chitchat or lingering after the deed is done. "When it's over, it's over," Julius insists.

Still, the emotional distance isn't such that it compels him to use condoms. With all the time he's spent in and around social service programs, he knows more about HIV and sexually transmitted diseases than most people. He knows, for instance, that since he's more often than not a bottom—the receptive partner in anal sex—his risk is heightened; HIV is far more easily transmitted through the porous lining of the anus than through the relatively resilient skin of the penis. Yet he figures he uses a condom maybe one in five times he has sex. "Why?" He shrugs helplessly and draws a blank. "It boggles my mind." His risk-calculation formula, however, is uncomplicated: if the guy puts on a rubber, he's cool with it; if not, same difference.

"There was a month that I was just like a sex machine," he recalls, "almost every day—until I got sick. I had like a high fever, all that shit. I thought I caught something." Often, a couple of weeks after someone contracts HIV that person will have symptoms that feel like the flu or mononucleosis. That's the brief, acute stage of HIV infection, where the virus replicates by the billions a day as the immune system ramps up its counterattack. HIV-prevention campaigns ominously advertise this physiological red flag in ads published in gay periodicals and posted in gay neighborhoods around the city: Are you sure it's just the flu? The idea is to draw people into testing, and thereby either catch a new infection before it spreads to someone else or to shock people into being more safe next time. The intervention, as such things are called in public health parlance, worked for Julius, for a while. "I got my results and I was fine," he explains with relief. "I said, maybe that's a warning! So I stopped for two weeks."

Julius is again at an uncharacteristic loss for words when asked to explain why he has so much sex in the first place.

"It's an escape," he suggests, conceding that he's certainly not just so horny that he needs casual sex three times a week. "And the funny thing is I do create some sort of attachment with these people—I mean, they e-mail me *so* much—and then I neglect them. Why? I don't know. I don't develop much attachment, but it's almost like I make them get attached to me."

So around seven or eight o'clock he chooses one of his would-be paramours to spend the early evening with. He rolls a joint and glides out onto Crystal Street. Julius is hyperaware of his homosexuality when walking through East New York. The easy swish that draws him welcome attention in other settings feels misplaced here, the sidelong glances tossed his way seem piercing rather than longing. It's the way he dresses, he figures, the way he color-coordinates his outfits and squeezes into one-size-too-small tank tops and jeans. "I'm always dressed up like, you can tell that child's a faggot from a mile away. From the way I walk, you can just *tell*," he says with a sigh. "I'm so self-conscious. Even when I sit on the train. I always read something. I always read a book so people don't look at my face."

Not that he's cowering in anything like a closet, or that he'd ever even consider such a thing possible. Indeed, it's his very refusal—even inability—to be discreet about his sexuality that's the problem. He's just out of place in East New York, and unable to conceal the ugly fact of it. So he walks briskly as he travels up Crystal and makes his way over the few harrowing blocks he must travel to the subway, and he tries to project strength, if not masculinity.

· ▪ ▪

East New York has long been the sort of place people conjure when imagining postapocalyptic urban worlds. The sprawling neighborhood sits on the far eastern edge of Brooklyn's land-locked central corridor, a vast urban interior that connects the borough's Atlantic Ocean beaches to the ring of cosmopolitan enclaves that creep inward from the East River. As Manhattan-ites spill farther into Brooklyn in search of deals on old brown-stones, increasing swaths of central Brooklyn are agonizing over the push and pull of development and gentrification. Man-ny's Prospect Park neighborhood and the bordering Bedford-Stuyvesant (once nicknamed "Do or Die Bed-Stuy") are today in the throes of volatile economic and racial change. But East New York, which is just east of Bed-Stuy, doesn't yet have such lofty problems. Few come to East New York other than those who al-ready live here; it's been that way for decades.

The neighborhood in fact offers a textbook study in how banks, real estate brokers, and urban planners in cities around the country worked in concert throughout the civil rights era to make sure American communities remained segregated. As Brooklyn historian and housing researcher Walter Thabit has documented, at the start of the 1960s, East New York was 85 percent white. By the end of 1966 the area had become 80 per-cent black and Puerto Rican. The change was neither coinci-dental nor harmless; the fearful, uncertain world that Julius clutches his pocketknife and sprints through each day was man-ufactured by greed.

East New York's initial growth came during the early twentieth-century industrial boom. New subway lines enabled working-class New Yorkers to live outside the commercial core, and freshly sprouting factories provided outer-ring jobs, so lower Manhattan's Italian and Jewish immigrants drifted into central Brooklyn, swelling its ranks over the years until it was a solidly white and lower-middle-class neighborhood by the time of the Depression. It wasn't until the postwar years that the area's demographics began shifting, as city planners flushed blacks and Puerto Ricans out of Manhattan's Upper West Side, where the tiny, one-room hovels landlords were cramming colored folks into had led to overcrowding in the neighborhood and angered white residents. So, like the Italian and Jewish immigrants before them, these migrants from the American South and Caribbean came to Brooklyn in search of better housing than they had in Manhattan, but what they found was still more predation.

Banks, realtors, and landlords recognized the chance for profit in segregation. Emboldened by pseudoscience theories about the inevitability of white flight, they launched the twin processes of "redlining" and "blockbusting." As blacks and Puerto Ricans moved into an area, the banks redlined those blocks, refusing to lend money to its building owners. Unable to renovate or even keep up their properties, landlords either dumped them on slumlords or became slumlords themselves. The slumlords, like their Upper West Side predecessors, hustled white tenants out and filled their buildings with black and Puerto Rican ones—whom they charged higher rents and offered fewer services, taking advantage of the limited housing options available to nonwhite renters in a segregated market. The affected areas quickly became overcrowded and the properties run down. Abandoned buildings spread as landlords left them to rot; arson erupted as property owners tried to salvage their investments with insurance claims. (There were fourteen hundred fires in East New York in 1965, four hundred of them in abandoned buildings.) All of this tore the community's social fabric in the same way it had in uptown Manhattan. Realtors stepped into this volatile mix with blockbusting tactics meant to push jittery whites out of the area to make room for overpriced sales to desperate black and Puerto Rican buyers. They papered blocks with flyers warning whites that it was "time to sell" and get out while they could. Brokers drastically lowballed white owners who called to ask about selling, further priming fears about property devaluation, then went door to door offering quick cash buyouts.

It worked. On some East New York blocks, according to Thabit's research, 30 to 40 percent of properties would flip in a year during the 1960s. The black and Puerto Rican buyers paid too-high prices for these properties and were forced to rent out their upper floors, necessarily to poorer families often on public assistance, further overcrowding the neighborhood and concentrating poverty there. Racial tension among the whites who stayed and the new black and Puerto Rican residents raged, culminating in massive rioting and street battles in the late '60s, which sounded the area's death knell. A ghetto had been born, along with all of the economic depravation that comes with it; 40 percent of East New York households were living in poverty by that point.

By the time Lionel and his friends bought their house, East New York had slogged through more than forty years of this orchestrated deterioration. Arsoned buildings had been either left to rot or torn down; vast swaths of empty lots filled with trash and rubble lay in their place. What few businesses operate in the area today are low end and hodgepodge—tire-repair shops, nail salons and barbershops, tiny dollar stores, and Chinese food joints with Plexiglas separating the operators from the customers. The unemployed young men who have long strolled up and down the neighborhood's blocks find plenty of work in the underground economy, however, from the drug trade to the various scams and hustles that keep New York City's neighborhoods buzzing. You run an off-the-books restaurant out of your house; you ride the subway and peddle everything from pirated DVDs to boxes of candy bars; and you jack other people's stuff to resell. In 2006 Lionel's precinct was still among twenty in the city with more than two thousand major felonies a year, and central Brooklyn was home to seven of the city's seventeen precincts with more than ten murders. The rows of apartment buildings like those along Crystal are run-down enough that the neighborhood is still in the city's top ten for complaints to the buildings department. By just about any measure, in fact, East New York is among the city's most worn-down locales: A quarter of the food-service businesses failed health inspection in 2005; the infant mortality rate was almost twice that of the city at large; Lionel's was among the top six neighborhoods for numbers of people receiving public assistance, two of which were in central Brooklyn.

"When I was a kid this neighborhood, for me, was scary," says Carlos, a stout but soft-spoken twenty-five-year-old Puerto Rican. He was one of a number of young gay East New Yorkers who started hanging around the Crystal Street house after Julius and the other queer kids moved in there.

Carlos is describing a peculiar fear, one rooted in familiarity rather than the unknown. Unaffiliated bystanders in the era's open-air drug markets were never targets of the often deadly violence, but they could nonetheless get caught in the crossfire—becoming accidental prisoners inside the battles of well-known, and often loved, combatants. "We knew a lot of the people that worked on the drugs. We knew a lot of people who were doing bad things, who were in the community. And they might have been family members as well, you know, but they contributed to that." Carlos shrugs. "You couldn't really enjoy yourself. As a child, you had to be cautious." One day his mom surprised him with a new bike, and he raced outside to troll the streets. He pedaled down the block and found himself in the middle of a shootout. Two young men were barreling toward him, each firing their gun at the other. "I loved the bike, but I just threw it and ran," Carlos remembers, first laughing at the absurdity of it, then sobering. "It was hard to be able to enjoy life in general as a child."

Geographic proximity notwithstanding, this whole scene couldn't be more distant from the iconic gay neighborhoods of New York, with their cute boutiques selling rainbow tchotchkes and designer clothes. In 2007 there were are at least five gay community publications in New York City; none circulated in East New York. Hundreds of businesses target gay New Yorkers—from bars to coffee shops to bookstores—and nowadays they can afford to specialize even further, with a number catering to black and Latino queers in search of their own aesthetic. None do business in East New York. One of the world's largest and most visible gay pride parades unfolds yearly just a thirty-minute subway ride from Carlos's front door, but he was twenty-five years old before the idea struck him that the event may be for him, too.

It was Lionel who planted that oddly radical seed. In meeting young people like Carlos and Julius, Lionel and his housemates became more and more aware of the need to offer them some sort of space in which to just stop and think, about their lives and their relationships and where they've been and where they were going. It didn't happen in any deliberate fashion, but rather case by case. One person would move in, then bring her friend, who'd tell his friend, and so on.

When Lionel and his partners bought the house, they'd really just been trying to break out of their collective ruts. They were young idealists and had all spent plenty of time working in urban do-gooder jobs, picking their way through the non-profit groups that try to fill in the spaces from which the public sector has shrunk and into which the private sector will not advance. But this business of saving the world had proved too often dispiriting—the jobs rarely encouraged the sort of bold moves that could really make a difference; they asked for long hours and offered little pay; and, worst of all, they were too often controlled by white liberals more interested in tending to their own pathos and guilt than ceding enough personal or collective privilege to allow black and brown folks a real chance. So the trio thought to start something up on their own.

And anyway, they all needed a place to live. Two of them were being kicked out of the apartment they shared. And after things fell apart with Lionel's latest girlfriend, he'd lost a place to stay, too. So when they came across this relatively affordable house, they pooled their money and credit and tossed their hats into New York City's raucous housing market. Their plan was to circle the wagons and figure out how to do some truly meaningful community organizing for once.

"The work that we want to do is not just 'organizing' as this narrow kind of thing," Lionel offers, launching into an explanation as unstructured as the idea itself, a vision that lands somewhere between hippie-style personalized politics and a more edgy invective against white supremacy. "It's about learning how to live, about healing. And what we wanted to do was to create a way to do organizing work and deal with police brutality and deal with gentrification and deal with the amount of trauma that we've been through, but focusing on healing. Looking at the different ways in which we are divided, with various identities and isms and all that. But not approach it from this hierarchical place. Just look at it. No doubt, I'm a fucking man and I got all the gender shit and this and that, but at the same time there's other things that make my life difficult and ways that the system is set up against me. So we tried to create someplace where we could dialogue, build trust, and heal ourselves while we deal with those differences."

But the first challenge they faced wasn't nearly so ethereal: they had to make friends with the neighbors, who had little reason to befriend or even trust a bunch of relatively privileged twenty- and thirty-somethings who came from somewhere other than East New York. "Everybody here knew everybody. They either grew up here on the block, or on the next block," says Lionel, who himself grew up in a middle-class family in Queens. "For the first two weeks, I don't think we left the front stoop. Because we knew that was gonna make or break us. They were either gonna burn the house down and make our lives miserable, or we were gonna become a part of this block."

In the process, Lionel started the slow, fretful process of coming out, a movement that was sped along by his new girl-friend.

Hermone met Lionel and the Crystal Street crew a few months after they bought the house. Like them, she was at her wit's end with the nonprofit world—she'd just been chased out of a job running skills-building programs for primarily black streetworkers in Brooklyn, because she tried to turn the thing into a collective, which pissed off the white executive director. That's Hermone's thing, turning stuff into collectives. She was just twenty-one years old when she met the folks from Crystal Street, but she'd already spent a lot of time on protest front-lines raging against the machine, and she was over that sort of ac-tivism too. "There came a time where I was like, all right, I'm tired of protest," she explains as she scoops her lush mane of shoulder-length dreadlocks back behind her neck, revealing a soft baby face that's incongruent with that of the seasoned organizer her resume describes. "I'm tired of the rah-rah bring-down-the-system bullshit. Because that's who I became, I be-came an act of defiance. And the reality is that an act of defiance is still constructed by the very things that make that defiance necessary." She speaks softly and deliberately, such that her words roll out with the meditative air you'd expect of someone who specializes in things like herbal treatments and tarot card readings. But she also conveys a passion that's almost unset-tling in its earnestness. She looks you in the eye when you talk, not as a negotiating ploy but because she assumes whatever you're saying is important to you and she thus wants to hear it. "You cannot transform something that you are fighting. You can't. You have to tap into the part of *you* that is part of that energy too, and transform it into something else." The best way to do that, she figures, is by rebuilding communities relationship by relationship, person by person, until there's critical mass for real change. The white lady at the streetworkers' group didn't get that; Lionel and these East New York cats did, and that was a turn-on.

Literally. Her and Lionel fell in fast love.

The couple made for a strange image given that Hermone is the sort of lesbian one would call a poster child. She roughs up her otherwise pretty-girl face and body with tattoos, piercings, and tight tank tops; she prefers dating not just women but dyke-identified, butch lesbians. As she puts it, "Most of the women I talk to are straight-up bulldaggers." But it was actually the maturity of her sexual identity that made her give the charge she felt with Lionel a chance. She was toying around with the burgeoning sexual and gender politics of being "two-spirited," which breaks down the usually rigid categories of gay/straight, male/female to let whatever happens, happen. So why not date a guy? Plus, they were palling around like close siblings, connecting in a way she had rarely felt with anyone. She dove on in.

And it wasn't just about Lionel, either: all four of the Crystal Street house's initial residents were grooving together, sorting through all of their evolving personal and political selves. "It steered into really intense encounters and we kind of fell in love with each other and went into dyke mode," Hermone jokes, mocking the caricature of lesbian couples plunging into intense relationships after a single meeting. " 'Oh, you gotta move in.' "

It was a big step for her, though. She'd been in constant motion throughout her short life—born in Ethiopia, fled with her family to Croatia when the war started, eventually landing in the U.S., where she'd continued shuttling around. The pattern repeated in her personal life. She had no problem plugging into things, but she rarely stayed around too long, she was always ready to move on to the next thing. "I was impossible to pin down. I was like that cat searching around for a home."

So maybe Crystal Street would be it, she figured. Maybe this would be home. It wouldn't be long before she and Lionel started bumping up against unexpected growths in both of their sexual and political identities, one driven by their commitment to share the home they were creating with similarly rootless kids like Julius and Carlos and, eventually, Manny.

THREE

Home, at least as a tangible place one inhabits, has always been foreign to Manny. Cassandra didn't mean to get pregnant back in 1985. At forty, she was an ambitious, black Puerto Rican woman in the process of remaking her life, beating the proverbial odds. She studied social work as a graduate student in Manhattan, and made do with an affordable one-bedroom flat way down in Staten Island. She was out for a jog one day when she met Manny's father. She hit it off with the dashing Jamaican man and, as such flings go, one thing rapidly led to another. As Manny understands the story, his biological parents went out on a couple of dates, had sex, and created him. It was an outcome Cassandra found herself wholly unprepared to deal with.

What happened next isn't a topic Manny and his mom discuss much; he says his efforts to do so have always been met with a stony silence. "She just couldn't afford to take care of me, I guess," Manny ventures, adding, "Well, it's all kind of fuzzy." What's clear is that she allowed a young white friend to take her toddler home with him to London. They faked a birth certificate declaring the man, Christian, to be Manny's adoptive father and shuttled him off to a whole different world. Christian was the son of a wealthy British politician, and he provided Manny an early life overflowing with privilege. Christian was also a semi-closeted gay man whose conservative family welcomed neither his homosexuality nor his new black baby. One of Manny's most vivid memories from those early years is of how Christian's father demonstrated the boy's difference from the rest of the family. "We were with one of the horses my grandfather had," Manny recalls, "and it was an ugly horse. It was black, but it was ugly! It had spots on it, and all these things. He pointed at it and he was like, 'Look, it's your brother.' "

The arrangement lasted longer than anybody was comfortable with, and after Manny finished up second grade Christian packed them up to rejoin Cassandra in New York. The trio piled into an artist's loft on Manhattan's West Side—in the then-still-seedy Meatpacking District—and tried failingly to, as Manny now puts it, do "the nuclear family thing." It was an odd setting for such an experiment. For decades, the Meatpacking District formed the northern border of a long stretch of dilapidated real estate on Manhattan's Lower West Side that hosted infamous scenes in the gay-male sexual revolution. A now-gone elevated highway ran along the Hudson River, and shipping trucks parked underneath it at night. On warm-enough evenings, men from all over the region flocked to the area and transformed it into a public sex playground. Meanwhile, hidden inside the Meatpacking District's maze of streets and processing plants was one of the most celebrated gay sex clubs of the late 1970s and early 1980s, called the Mineshaft, where men acted out the pre-AIDS era's leather and S&M sexual theater. Like the young men in Brooklyn's Prospect Park years later, gay men in '70s-era New York claimed all of this space as theirs. Positioned as it was on the outskirts of mainstream New York, the Meatpacking District offered a privacy and security that remained essential; the space was ignored and forgotten by the rest of society after dark, and thus provided an empty stage on which gay men could safely revel in a sexually defined and still-disapproved-of social scene.

By the time an eight-year-old Manny moved there in the mid-

1990s, the Meatpacking District's countercultural milieu was more history than present. Still, the stylish restaurants and straight nightclubs that dominate the neighborhood today had not yet fully replaced its slaughterhouses, with their stench of dead flesh filling the air and creeks of blood leaking into the narrow, cobblestone streets. Stilettoed women still teetered up to johns rather than doormen. And for one of the few times he'd experience in his youth, Manny's already palpable sense of being an outsider felt appropriate to him.

He didn't, however, know what to make of his aspiring parents—the hardworking, if hip, mom he'd spent summers with in Puerto Rico and New York cut an awkward figure next to the funky yet urbane white man he'd called dad for eight years. The pair never succeeded in quieting the dissonance of their lives. "My dad's friends would come over and he would hug them, be affectionate," Manny remembers. "There was none of that between my mom and dad." He understood they were not lovers, and never had been. Still, he wanted them to love each other more. Cassandra and Christian had been better friends once, but Manny believes her decision to give him up spawned a steadily festering guilt, which in turn emotionally walled her off first from her old friend and, eventually, from Manny, too. He sensed this distance at the time, and throughout his early childhood, but he never made too much out of it. "I didn't resent her," he says, "yet."

Manny's mom enrolled him in third grade at a Catholic elementary school in Brooklyn's Park Slope neighborhood, just blocks away from the park where he and Jason would turn tricks not too many years later. The school was a far cry from the proto-chic Meatpacking District, and Manny figures that was the point for Cassandra—to reground her son in tradition. Manny, however, hated everything about the place. The hideous uniforms of yellow oxfords with green ties and pants made him look like a black leprechaun. He cringed under the authority of the bossy nuns from the moment they'd ring the bell ordering kids to line up in the courtyard to the day's merciful end. He felt no kinship with the school's primary population of kids from working-class Italian and Haitian families. So, feeling out of place, he pre-emptively played up his differences rather than hide them, emphasizing his on-again, off-again British accent and affecting a preppy, aesthete air he'd always maintain in some form. The results were predictable. "I got called 'fag' a lot," he says with a shrug.

But most of all Manny hated the religious element of the school. He already considered himself too worldly and rational to take the romantic leap of believing a man he never knew had died for sins he hadn't yet committed. And he particularly detested the Communions, in which kids were instructed to pay homage to traditional ideas about mom, dad, and family, things that didn't make such tidy sense to him.

All of this led Manny to act out—flashes of anger, impertinent behavior, blowing off any work that didn't engage him. School administrators eventually decided his antics were more than growing pains, and directed Cassandra to send him for a psychiatric evaluation. "This is when my issues with my mom started," Manny explains. He posits the school problems inflamed her smoldering maternal insecurities, triggering a fear that someone would decide she was an unfit mother and report her to the city. Whatever the impetus, Cassandra began reclaiming supremacy in Manny's life.

So the summer after third grade, Cassandra loaded Manny onto the E train and led him out to Queens for a few days' worth of tests to determine how and why the kid was so unstable. For Manny it was all a welcome adventure, at first.

It was the longest subway ride he'd ever taken, and he hunkered down in the last car for a wide-eyed view of the city's bowels trailing behind the train as it rumbled out to St. John's

University. The tangled arteries of New York's subway system are a uniquely democratic public space in America. Around 4.5 million people shuffle through the system every day, coming and going through all walks of life. It's one of few places where Wall Street brokers must rub shoulders with high school kids from the Bronx, where white-collar workers interact with hipster artists, where young black men and middle-aged Polish women and undocumented Mexican laborers and all manner of the city's 8-million-member mishmash come together in a jumble of humanity, each forced to look another in the face and acknowledge, if not always understand, an existence beyond their own. But the system's dense map of colored, numbered, and lettered trains also draws a hieroglyphic of New York's racial and economic geography. Each subway line has its own flavor, informed by the communities it chugs through, and the blue A/C/E line that Manny would ride his whole life is, arguably, the most *colored*. It runs through central Brooklyn neighborhoods like East New York, up along Manhattan's West Side, and on into black Harlem and Latino Washington Heights. As you ride along, the underground economy that fuels those neighborhoods bustles, too, with young men and women hustling everything from their self-produced hip-hop CDs to incense and scented oils to boxes of M&Ms. Teens clear narrow openings in the jammed aisles and perform stunt-dance acrobatics for money; dreadlocked Rastas set up stools and pound out drum-circle routines, passing the hat during station stops.

The E train is the outlier in this subway cluster. Watching from the rear window, a young Manny saw entirely new realms pass in his wake when the E veered off from the pack at Times Square, darted eastward across the city's midsection, and plunged under the East River. It came up into the immigrant neighborhoods of Queens, home to the nation's most ethnically diverse county, and he watched as the urban density he was coming to know at home and school slowly gave way to working-class suburbs of modest single-family homes and duplexes, mixed in with massive complexes of apartments and condos. All the way at the end of the line—a thirty-minute ride from the heart of Manhattan and a world apart—sits St. John's leafy, classically collegiate campus.

Manny and Cassandra arrived and were making their way across the campus when he spied members of the school's Division I basketball team practicing. He lit up with unexplainable excitement at their towering masculine and universally dark bodies ripe with exertion. Enchanted, he convinced his mom to walk a circuitous route that took them nearer to the courts and allowed a closer look. He watched the squad run drills for as long as Cassandra permitted, and begged her to bring him back after the interview. He wasn't sure exactly what he wanted from the young men, but his desire was unmistakable. "I wanna hang out with *them,*" he remembers thinking.

Social and biological scientists alike have fussed over what makes someone homosexual. The proverbial nature-versus-nurture debate divides human sexuality into competing camps —one professing you're born with a particular inclination for same- or opposite-sex attraction, the other arguing that environment at least helps shape eros. But the meaning society has drawn from these competing theories hasn't been static. The Western world's preoccupation with explaining homosexuality took root at the turn of the twentieth century, when the idea that same-sex sexual desire was congenital first gained prominence. Today, gay folks and their political and cultural allies often argue that people are born homosexual or bisexual—just like they're born hetero—and thus that these are all equally natural and irreproachable desires. Autopsy studies seeking to prove the point in the early 1990s found a cluster of brain cells in homosexual men to be larger than those of heterosexual men, touching off speculation about neurological determinants. Another theory, floated later in the '90s, cited differences in the ear canals of men and women and noted that lesbians have aural physiology more akin to men than to their straight peers. Conservative researchers pooh-poohed these and other claims to the biology of homosexuality at the time, but at the century's outset the roles were reversed: those favoring a biological answer then considered homosexuality simply one of many inherited birth defects, and doctors explored all manner of medical perversion to cure it—castrations, hysterectomies, lobotomies.

As the century progressed and the notion of a normative libido further developed, theories about homosexuality's cause shifted from the body to the mind. The science of the mind gained a place in America's popular consciousness during World War II, when the armed forces subjected incoming soldiers to psych exams, and by the war's end the nation had largely embraced the field's infallibility. So as years of wartime upheaval gave way and the zeitgeist turned to the stable comfort of tradition, psychiatry helped to reestablish norms around age, gender, and sexuality, among other things. Psychiatrists kicked around a wide range of causal theories for homosexuality, though all maintained the assumption of pathology. Gender confusion was key: a kid like Manny could have been coddled too much by his mom, or failed to learn manhood by having as a primary male role model someone like Christian. The potential for criminality was also central: due to their pathology, both Manny and Christian would have been considered latent sexual predators, or perhaps Manny's own deviance could be explained through uncovering hidden abuse by Christian.

By the close of the 1970s, all major psychiatric and psychological professional groups had abandoned these notions and agreed homosexuality was not a pathology, and they had narrowed the putative disorder in clinical manuals. But "gender dysphoria"—in which a boy or girl can't act appropriately for their gender—remains among the list of disorders in 2007.

And even the theories dealing explicitly with homosexuality die hard in popular imagination: when a Republican congress-member was infamously caught flirting with male teen pages during the 2006 elections, he explained his behavior, in part, by citing childhood abuse by a priest.

As for the grade-schooler Manny, as he stood courtside leer-ing at the St. John's University basketball team, he didn't then and doesn't now care much about why or how he came to desire the players' impressive physiques. Whatever the cause, the feel-ings were unequivocally real, as tangible as his own skin, and the plain fact of their existence generated neither shame nor pride. But what Manny lacked, and would continue to lack for years, was an understanding of what those feelings meant to larger society and a strategy for sorting through everyone else's prepackaged meanings to find his own. These are the questions that would bedevil him; like many of today's queer youth, Manny's preoccupation wouldn't be what he felt or why he felt it, but rather how to live with it. For now, however, he just liked what he saw. "I was like, 'Oh my God! That's a boy—and I like it!'"

When Cassandra and Manny finally arrived at the office where his evaluation was to take place, the fun suddenly stopped. The room was littered with colorful pictures and building blocks, but those weren't for Manny; he was asked instead to do math—a hateful subject. Things got worse once the woman began in-terrogating his mother. The middle-aged white lady sat perched across the desk, asking question after question about their fam-ily and his upbringing. Manny listened—puzzled and not a lit-tle annoyed—as his mother rewrote his life history.

When the woman asked about Manny's childhood, his mom spoke as if his adoptive father never existed. She described her-self as a single mother, working and studying and trying to keep above water while raising Manny alone. She professed that he'd not only been born in the city but raised there his whole life. Manny in turn piped up and proudly pointed out that he'd lived abroad with his adoptive father. Cassandra demurred. "Well, I've lived here for fifteen years. And Manny has lived here part of that time. Sometimes his aunt comes from Puerto Rico to take care of him. He loves my rice and beans."

"No I don't," Manny protested, disgusted at the thought.

Cassandra silenced him with a soft rub on his head.

Underlying all of these fibs was Cassandra's desire to yank her child back—by any means necessary—into the black, Puerto Rican world of which she was a proud member. Cassandra had come to New York in the early 1970s, looking for more education and work opportunities than she'd had back home. In so doing, she joined a long and massive wave of Puerto Rican migration that dramatically reshaped New York City. For many Americans, that migration's relevance stops with Baseball Hall of Famer Roberto Clemente. But the Puerto Rican influx into New York is a remarkable bit of American history. The movement began in 1945, when there were just thirteen thousand Puerto Ricans in the city; by the following year there were more than fifty thousand. They kept coming, at the pace of twenty-five thousand a year, and by the 1990 Census, Puerto Ricans were 12 percent of the city's population.

Puerto Rico sits about midway along the string of islands that run from Florida's southern tip to the top of South America, and it's been a U.S. possession since America claimed it at the end of the Spanish-American War in 1898. (More specifically, in 1917 the U.S. anointed Puerto Rico's residents American citizens—albeit ones who to this day have no voting representative in Congress.) Spain had forced the island into a limited agricultural economy based largely on sugarcane farming; American companies took over the industry's reins and drove the economy into still narrower realms. The move sparked huge economic growth, but the benefits were limited to the American capitalists and their few local managers. The job market actually shrank, and by the 1930s unemployment was around 65 percent. So Puerto Ricans began looking for better opportunities on the mainland—a search that was still ongoing when Cassandra struck out four decades later.

The midcentury migration in particular reshaped not only New York's racial demographics but also its geography. As successive planeloads of Puerto Ricans arrived, the owners and planners of the city's housing stock sensed a chance to get rich. During the mid-1940s rush, rental agents chartered buses to meet inbound flights and ship the hordes directly off to the small, poorly kept tenements and single-room apartments on Manhattan's Upper West Side—in a precursor to the predation that would later rip up East New York. Fortunes were made cramming Puerto Rican families into these high-rent, low-maintenance structures. According to Walter Thabit, one infamous landlord increased his take from around $100,000 to nearly $300,000 in a single year, using the well-tested strategy of chopping his building up into small, overpriced and under-maintained single-room units.

And as would happen in Brooklyn, while landlords got rich, the area's social fabric tore under the stress of overcrowding and concentrated poverty. Middle-class whites already living in the area grew angry with the rapid demographic shift and began to claim rises in crime, to demand the city do something. In the late 1950s the city finally responded and began a series of redevelopment projects, displacing thousands of low-income blacks and Puerto Ricans in the process. Thus began the black and Puerto Rican migration toward the growing stock of affordable housing in central Brooklyn neighborhoods like the one Manny and Cassandra would later call home.

It wasn't long after the psych evaluation that Cassandra and Manny took a day to hang out together in the park, but instead of going up to Central Park, which was closer to home, they took a trip out to Brooklyn, by his school. They set up camp in the large, open field that anchors Prospect Park, relaxing on its rolling hills among the potpourri of families that typically fill the space. Several communities abut the park, but it is flanked to the east by neighborhoods that have long been home to working-class black and brown people, particularly immigrants from the Caribbean. New Orleans and its Mardi Gras are perhaps most popularly associated with the Afro-Caribbean diaspora in America, but Eastern Parkway makes the most credible claim at being its heart. Brooklyn is home to the world's largest population of Caribbean expats, and the annual Labor Day festival celebrating that fact has been said to draw as many as 3 million revelers to Eastern Parkway.

Cassandra and Manny spent a rare day of out-and-about mother-son time and it was a nice change. Days with Cassandra were often mundane, hanging around at home with her being more parent than pal. Today was different. They'd played in a strange new park, and it'd been nice. But as the sun went down on their afternoon and the pair packed up, things turned weird. "My mother's like, 'Let's go home,'" Manny recalls. "But we weren't walking toward the train station." He sensed something was wrong, that there'd been a sudden change in the day's casual vibe and that the odd route they were taking was about something more than choosing an alternative way back to Manhattan. They left the park and made their way across the large, multilane roundabout that redirects traffic to accommodate the oasis. They turned down Eastern Parkway and walked past the library and the botanical gardens and the museum and, when they were still several blocks short of another subway train that could have taken them back to Manhattan, they stopped in front of the building in which Cassandra planned, unbeknownst to him, to start their lives again.

"What are we doing here?" Manny asked, his alarm piquing. There was no answer.

Something told him to flee, but as the tears started flowing

Cassandra scooped him up and carried him into the elevator. He was too big for her to handle easily, and they struggled as she lugged him across the sparse lobby's black-and-white checkered tile and onto the elevator. She dragged him into the apartment, got him into his new room, and shut the door, leaving him to thrash about until he cried himself to sleep. "It was fully furnished," he explains, recalling a detail that cemented the event in his mind as a carefully planned ambush. He awoke the next morning to the smell of his mother's cooking, staring out the window at the novelty of foliage. Manny and Cassandra would never fully discuss the move, or why she felt the need to orchestrate it so abruptly. Today, he suspects she meant well. He figures that she and Christian agreed a hard break would somehow make more sense to his young mind than a slog through the confusing details of their dissolving arrangement—the weird mix of impulse and practicality that initially drove them together; Manny's poor fit in London and Cassandra's nagging guilt in New York, which prompted their family-making efforts in the Meatpacking District; the inescapable reality that an independent Cassandra could scarcely afford, financially or emotionally, to stay in Manhattan. In the end, Manny understood only enough to discard any traditional idea of home and family. He sighs at the memory. "Everything changed. Whether or not I liked rice and beans, that's what I was eating."

Manny was actually no stranger to Puerto Rican culture. He'd spent many childhood summers on the island. Cassandra would take him to stay with her mother and sister in their old family home near Ponce, the island's second largest city, where they owned a modest house with a nice backyard in the Ponce suburbs. And it was there, in the summer after sixth grade, that Manny figured out what it was he had wanted from those hulking basketball players at St. Johns.

Cassandra's brother was more financially successful than

his sisters or his mother. He made good money in real estate and had moved his family into a big house about a twenty-minute drive down the coast. Visiting them was never much fun to Manny. They put on stuffy airs to match their wealth, and were far more traditional than the rest of the family—there were more rules. But there was a bright side to the visits: cousin Nanuco.

They called him Nanuco after the name of a particularly pungent cologne he wore. He was a few years older than Manny, in the peak of puberty, and his caramel skin stretched over a body rapidly morphing from boy to man. He and Manny were the only two boys in the lot, so Nanuco took his younger cousin under his wing as a little brother. "As the, like, masculine, person in my life," Manny haltingly explains, "even when I was younger, he'd always taken it upon himself to, I don't know, do those things that you do. You know? He wanted to teach me how to shave."

Manny, in turn, certainly looked up to Nanuco—but not in a brotherly way. They'd roughhouse and wrestle, and the gripping and pulling of contact would light Manny's body into flames. He wanted much more than a sibling's love from his cousin.

One day the family took a weekend trip a few hours down the coast to a favored beach. Because Ponce is on the southern coast, separated by a mountain range from the eastern resorts and the cruise ships docking in San Juan, Ponceños—as southern Puerto Ricans are known—can vacation there without fighting the throngs of Western holiday makers and the accompanying high prices. The area's white-sand beaches stretch along water calm enough to swim in, and it's often possible to pick your way inland and find secluded ponds. So one afternoon during the family's trip, Nanuco and Manny set off from the beach in search of inland adventure.

They found a nearby pond and Nanuco stripped down naked and dove in. Manny followed behind. He was in heaven watching Nanuco's burgeoning musculature splash around, and as they swam and played, he felt his now-familiar desire rising inside. When they paused in the shallow water, squatting across from one another, he gave up trying to control his feelings. I want to kiss you, he thought to himself, and plunged blindly forward.

But he stumbled. He fell into Nanuco's lap and landed a kiss on his cousin's chest rather than his face.

That wasn't how Manny had imagined the moment; he pictured a romance like men and women have in the movies. Still, his brief horror was eased by the fact that Nanuco hadn't resisted, hadn't jumped out of the way or shoved him or throttled him for the gambit. Instead, he opened his legs slightly wider and allowed Manny to nestle closer in to him. Manny sat in the water and, emboldened, made a second play for a kiss. This one went as planned.

"This was it!" Manny remembers feeling, his body ringing with epiphany as the boys awkwardly made out. "We just kissed for like ten minutes," Manny says. "And then he ran off, and I ran off after him. So that was the beginning of our summer affair."

Thereafter, whenever Manny's mom brought him by his uncle's house, the boys would sequester themselves in Nanuco's bedroom, where they'd strip down and explore their bodies together. It never went beyond groping and kissing, but it was groundbreaking for Manny. And it wasn't his only fling that summer.

His family had long been friends with the neighbors who lived across the street from his grandmother and aunt's house. Their son, El, was the same age as Manny, and the two had spent summers playing together throughout their childhood. Manny had always been flirtatious, pushing the boundaries of what boys are supposed to do with one another. They'd play hide-and-seek and he'd tag El by grabbing his ass; El rarely objected. But after the day in the pond with Nanuco, Manny dropped all pretense of gender-appropriate play. He came up with a new game: Sonic the Hedgehog, after the popular video game in which the hero Sonic chases down an evil villain. Manny's live-action version would end with the boys embracing and him grinding against El through their clothes. "I would dry hump him all day."

None of these encounters—not with Nanuco and not with El—gave Manny any pause. They just seemed natural—though he did know enough to be discreet. He knew, for instance, that since he and El played in the same bedroom he and his mom slept in, his mom could walk in at any time, so he never tried to get them undressed in the way he and Nanuco did. But shame never crossed his mind. "It wasn't something where I was like, 'Oh my God, I can't believe I'm doing this,'" Manny explains. "It was more like, 'Yeah!'"

Nanuco felt differently.

Near the end of the summer, Manny was visiting his uncle's house and eager for what he knew could be his last exploratory session with his cousin. He went into Nanuco's room and started getting undressed. He was lying on the bed, shirt off and pants soon to follow, when Nanuco walked in.

"Put your clothes on," he snapped.

"Huh? What?" Manny asked, confused and frightened by the sudden change in tone about their encounters. He realized Nanuco was serious, that something was wrong here, and he pleaded for a reprieve.

"But why?"

For Nanuco, this had all just been experimentation, part of the ongoing process of figuring out how to harness all the raging hormones and bizarre new feelings coursing through his body, and his experiment was complete. It had been interesting, perhaps, but now it was time to stop this kid stuff before it corrupted them both. He turned to Manny and masked his fear with exasperation.

"You know what they call that?"

"What?"

"Gay!"

The word fell like a wall between them, and Manny frantically raced to push it back up. "But we have fun," he begged.

His insistence must have frustrated Nanuco, and his cousin angrily drove home the consequences of their actions. "*Faggots*," he hissed, brandishing the slur they'd brought upon themselves.

As Manny stood there, naked from the waist up, he slowly fell into his second epiphany of the summer: his desires were shameful. He remembered hearing the same taunts at school, and for once put the disembodied words together with their meaning—a stark rebuke of the physical and emotional feelings he'd always so matter-of-factly considered. This was the reaction Nanuco had sought. "I think he was trying to help me. He was just being really big-brotherly: 'This is what they call it. It's not a good thing,' " Manny says now. "He wanted it to be a tender moment," he assures himself. "But it hurt."

Like broad swaths of American youth, Manny first encountered the word *faggot* at school. In a 2005 survey of just over seventeen hundred gay, lesbian, bisexual, and transgender students, eight out of ten reported hearing words like *faggot* and *dyke* used "often" or "frequently" at school by other kids. Nearly a fifth of those surveyed said they heard it from school personnel. Two-thirds reported being harassed themselves because of their sexual orientation, and nearly half said they got picked on because they didn't act appropriately boyish or girlish.

Still more common are phrases like *that's so gay* and *you're being queer*, which aren't directed at homosexuality itself but are simply meant to identify something as particularly bad—gayness and queerness standing as self-evidently awful enough ideas that they become catchall adjectives for anything unwanted. Nine out of ten students reported hearing these putdowns. They are widely considered innocuous because they aren't explicit slurs, but it turns out the kids who are actually gay and queer find them more difficult to dismiss—two-thirds of students in the survey felt stung by these sorts of remarks. Overall, 64 percent said they simply felt unsafe at school because of their sexual orientation.

The survey was conducted by the Gay, Lesbian, and Straight Education Network, or GLSEN. Founded by a gay teacher named Kevin Jennings in the early 1990s, GLSEN started as a school club where gay and straight kids got together to talk and figure out how not to be afraid of one another. It's grown into a national network of such clubs, known as gay-straight alliances, that spans all fifty states and works to make schools more safe and supportive places, not just for gay kids but for talking about sexuality and sexual identity in general. Each year, GLSEN surveys students and educators to measure the national climate for these sorts of conversations, and the results aren't heartening. On the most immediate level, teachers and administrators appear unwilling to intervene when students are bandying language that demeans gay people. Only 16 percent of students surveyed said that staff, on hearing homophobic remarks, "frequently" did something about it. But more broadly, GLSEN's surveys show schools doing very little to give kids like Manny perspective on the feelings they are having. More than 80 percent of the students said their schools taught nothing about gay people, their history or relevant events. That silence redounds for those who aren't likely to encounter this information elsewhere in their lives. Left with no broader reference point against which to measure their own experiences, isolated gay kids thrash about in everything from fruitless attempts at repression to outsize rebellions against the pressure to be what they are not, all in an effort to make sense of otherwise typically pubescent pains and passions.

The most obvious place to begin addressing all of this is in sex-education classes. Traditionally, sex ed has been a controversial subject among parents and educators alike, but the grounds of debate have shifted over the years. Polling shows that the once heated dispute over whether to have it at all is over. In 2003 the Kaiser Family Foundation, National Public Radio, and Harvard University's Kennedy School of Government polled seventeen hundred adults and found that just 7 percent believed sex education should not be taught in public schools. Today's debate turns instead on what topics should and should not be taught in these classes.

And on that score, the vast majority of people surveyed— three-quarters—felt that homosexuality was an appropriate enough topic. The majority of those people also wanted the subject dealt with neutrally—neither condoning nor condemning homosexuality, but rather just explaining what it is. Yet according to an Alan Guttmacher Institute study, as of 1998 only nine of the thirty-nine states that had policies regulating sex education made any mention of sexual orientation. In all but two of those, the rule either banned all discussion of homosexuality or required it be treated, in the think tank's words, as "abnormal or dangerous." (Massachusetts and New Jersey mandated that sexuality be discussed, but offered no content guidance.)

But in the years since the Guttmacher Institute study, a new fuss has erupted over just how much sex of any kind should come up in sex ed. Conservative activists who once opposed the whole enterprise have moved to co-opt it by promoting what is known as abstinence-only education. In this guise, sex ed teaches strictly the dangers of premarital sex, leaving out all discussion of contraception and other ways to lessen those dangers. According to the Kaiser/NPR/Harvard survey, abstinence-only is an unpopular idea: Just 15 percent of respondents thought it made sense. But once again there's a gulf between the beliefs of most Americans and the actions of school administrators, as the researchers found such programs in widespread use: nearly a third of middle school and high school sex-education curriculums were limited to abstinence as of 2003. Meanwhile, a congressionally mandated review of publicly funded abstinence-only programs, published in 2007 by Mathematica Policy Research, found that the programs had no impact on sexual behavior. Teens in the programs were equally as likely to have sex as peers who hadn't participated, started having sex at the same mean age (14.9 years) as their peers, and had the same number of lifetime sex partners. Of course, abstinence-only's premise that all nonmarital sex is dangerous also leaves gay kids two choices—never have sex, or accept a life of danger.

As Manny made his own way through middle school, New York was still among the states without a clear policy on abstinence or homosexuality. An early 1990s attempt to allow discussions about homosexuality in sex ed got then–schools chancellor Joseph Fernandez run out of office and made the whole topic of sex ed a political lightning rod that nobody wanted to touch. After years of uproar from AIDS and family planning activists, the education department finally updated the curriculum in 2005. The new version made information about STDs available at younger ages, but it also codified an emphasis on abstinence and declined to discuss sexual orientation beyond the context of HIV risk. The effect of all this is that the sexual education of gay kids like Manny gets relegated to the whims and judgments of the instructors they encounter.

That reality set up disaster for Manny, who sauntered back to school after his eventful summer in Puerto Rico with a new and demonstrable understanding of his sexuality. He was years behind his peers in this respect. At age twelve, Manny was just beginning to explore feelings and relationships that others had been urged throughout their lives to consider, in ways both explicit and implicit, from Ken and Barbie dolls straight through to pop radio romances. Manny understood that the newness of his sexual awareness set him apart from his peers, but he believed it made him more rather than less sophisticated, that he was now wiser and in even less need of whatever the school environment had to offer. So when his global studies teacher walked into class and introduced a unit on sex ed, Manny sighed wearily, thinking, What can you tell me that I don't already know?

"Today we're going to talk about sex," the teacher began. Manny remembers him as a study in gluttony—an insistently masculine middle-aged white man with a giant beer belly that groaned out over the top of his belt. "He would have smoked cigars if he could," Manny charges.

After quieting the adolescent uproar that followed his announcement, the teacher cued up an instructional film. Manny sank into his desk along the far wall, where he always sat, off center stage.

"We'll watch the film and if you have any questions, ask."

The film played, explaining reproductive physiology and how men and women have sex together. It covered sexually transmitted diseases, with lots of talk about the pitfalls of having sex before getting married. As Manny watched, he grew first alienated, then angry.

"Whatever is said in this room, stays in this room," the teacher pledged at the film's end, spurring discussion. "You can ask me anything."

Tentatively, the questions began to flow out. What's this STD and how's it differ from that STD? Explain more about the vagina. Manny was disgusted. Surely there's more, he thought. Surely someone gets that this is bullshit, that they're leaving out all of these intense feelings I've been having. Finally, someone broached the question, obliquely. "Is this the only way that people have sex?"

It's unclear whether Manny's peer was genuinely curious or just cheekily trying to stir up the conversation. Either way, their teacher quickly shut this particular line of questioning down. "Well, it's the way you're supposed to have sex."

Manny's emotions boiled over. He shot a stiff arm into the air to ask his own question, but when called on he found he had nothing to stay. Instead, he stood up, lifted his chair off the ground, and hurled it to the front of the room. It grazed past the teacher and slammed into the blackboard before bouncing and clanging its way across the floor and back toward the students. As the class sat in silent awe, Manny just stood there, his heart racing and his ears ringing with the echo of the chair's metal legs scraping the floor as he had snatched it up. "When I picked up the chair, it was like I was seeing so many different colors. I thought I was gonna black out, but I didn't."

The teacher's own rage quickly rose to meet Manny's. Sputtering, he managed just a gutteral "Get OUT!"

They were words Manny was glad to hear. He stormed out of the classroom, strode into the empty hallway, leaped down the stairs, and marched straight through the building's front door out into the Brooklyn afternoon. This blinding rage was increasingly familiar terrain for him, a defensive bunker into which he fled whenever the external context in which he found himself clashed too vividly with the internal narrative he was trying to construct. He'd already been kicked out of the dreadful Catholic elementary school for a similar eruption, and he fully expected this outburst to get him tossed from this latest school. But Manny's educational career would survive the incident, and he'd go on to matriculate from junior high the following year. It would, however, be his last graduation.

FOUR

"All I've known is this area," Carlos will tell you. "I really haven't come out of here." And it's a pretty literal truth. At twenty-five, he's spent his entire life inside a two-mile stretch of East New York. He's never traveled, not even to his family's native Puerto Rico. He makes the occasional sojourn into Manhattan, but it's as foreign as France. This stasis isn't a problem for Carlos, because East New York, for all its warts, offers everything he needs. It's the comforting nest of a well-known home.

That's in no small part because his whole family has always been found inside these few miles, too. For most of Carlos's life, they all lived in two adjacent apartment buildings on Gary Avenue. He's the youngest of five kids—two brothers and two sisters. They're all grown now, some married, but all have stayed nearby, along with uncles, cousins, and nieces and nephews. His mom married his stepfather, Armando, when Carlos was young. He never met his biological father—who's somewhere in Puerto Rico—and so considers Armando to be his dad, "because he raised me." They haven't always gotten along, however, mainly because Armando's a guy's guy, too often loud and swaggering. "He has that Puerto Rican thing," Carlos explains, letting out a quiet, self-conscious laugh that embodies the polar opposite aesthetic of the macho aura he's describing. Carlos has got the short, thick build of a fullback, and if he styled himself differently he could probably come off as a tough guy. But his tidy, clean-cut look; his light, freckled skin; and his rolling, singsong voice instead give off a delicacy and vulnerability unassociated with the machismo of his brothers and his father. "Older Puerto Ricans, they go to public places and they want to be seen, they want to be heard. I'm more like mellow, more laid back. And he'll conversate with me, but be looking directly at someone else. And I'm like, 'Conversate with me!' " But Carlos and Armando love each other across this communication divide. And Armando has always been good to Carlos's mom, always loved her. "He means well," Carlos succinctly concludes, in a typically earnest tone. "He's always worried about me. If I need anything, he'll do his best to make it happen for me." That's what's most important, because things have rarely been easy on Gary Avenue.

The family's challenges have drawn them close. The neighborhood drug trade and its accompanying violence were staples of Carlos's younger years, and that made his folks understandably protective. As the baby in a big clan, he got special treatment; everybody kept an eye out for him. But in his late teens, his mother's disabling illness slowly emerged—a schizophrenia that suddenly threw the family's stable life into chaos. Carlos's mom had actually shown signs of schizophrenia and depression his whole life, but her episodes were never bad enough that the family considered them to be anything more than just her personality quirks. They figured she was moody. "I knew my mom was kind of different, 'cause she could get angry very easily. She slept a lot sometimes," Carlos explains, then quickly rises to her defense. "She was a good mother. She took care of us. She fed us. You know? But"—he takes a breath, shrugs— "there were times that she'd slack off. And it was those issues that she had and was dealing with." So as a teen Carlos shifted from protected to protector, watching over his mother as she grew increasingly sick and standing in the maternal gap her disability left. Now he plans the family holiday parties, offers a confiding ear for everyone's life drama, helps siblings and cousins figure out complicated English-language paperwork, and generally holds court in the apartment he carefully designed and still shares with his mother and Armando.

While anybody else in this family of large personalities would feel stifled by the role, for Carlos it has been ideal. He is a caretaker by nature, as witnessed by the fact that he's lined the sunny front room of the family's frilly apartment with giant cages of exotic birds and a fish tank. But becoming the family matriarch has also been a great way to shrink his visibility, to not only keep others from looking too closely at his own life but to distract himself from doing so as well. For years, it gave Carlos just the cover he needed to balance his external and internal lives—by taking on everyone else's problems, he could maintain a place in his East New York world while figuring out the increasingly bizarre feelings he was having about sex and sexuality.

"As a kid, I always felt like I didn't fit in," Carlos explains. He did his best to roughhouse with the neighborhood boys, to play basketball in the streets and strut around in the way a young tough is expected to do. But in the end, he found the whole charade a bore. The real fun was hanging out and jabbering with the girls. "I mean, it was so much more interesting. They had so much more to talk about," he says with a laugh. So Carlos honed an ability to be both boy and girl. He could butch up and "be ghetto" when required, but let go and kick it with his girlfriends when the time was right. He didn't mind the split personality; he considered it a weapon in his social arsenal, frankly, one that allowed him to seamlessly navigate all of the neighborhood's different worlds.

Except that sometimes it would all get to be too much to sort out, and he'd find himself caught stumbling with his guard down. Like the first time he met that Keith kid. Carlos was

twenty-two at the time, and should have felt comfortably supe-
rior to the young thirteen-year-old. But there was something
about the way Keith looked at him, like he knew a secret.

Carlos was sitting on the stoop drinking beers and whiling
away the afternoon with his brothers and cousins when Keith
and a group of young girls rode by on their bikes. He'd seen the
kid around before, and always noticed his swishy style, the way
he'd let his hair grow long and shoot up in a wild, flamboyant
burst radiating out from his round, dark face; and how sometimes he'd even bind the thick hair up in a rag. Keith didn't seem
shy about the fact to Carlos: the guy preferred the life of a girl.

It being a slow summer day, Keith and the girls stopped
to size the guys up, which led the two camps to launch into the
age-old street-corner pastime of playing the dozens, boys versus
girls. The playful putdowns flew back and forth as the groups
tried to one-up one another with witty remarks. Carlos readily
chimed in from his perch on the boys' team, but noticed Keith
saying nothing. So he tried to bait the curious young man, who,
as he puts it, is "well proportioned in certain ways."

"Look at your big ass!" Carlos jibed. "I sure feel sorry for that
bike."

He immediately felt like he'd made a conspicuously odd
rhetorical choice by focusing such close attention on another
boy's ass, and he still blames the booze for making it "come
out that way." The rest of the group didn't take much notice,
but Keith's interest was piqued. Keith was normally a mouthy
ringleader in these sorts of exchanges. His reaction to Carlos's
remark, however, was simply continued silence—an uncomfortable silence made all the more so by the too-knowing look
he tossed. It was a ploy that said more than any verbal comeback
could have, and Carlos still squirms at the memory. "He just
stood quiet—and *looking* at me."

Carlos lived in terror of moments like these. It wasn't so
much that someone like Keith could see what he was hiding, but

more that the other guys could, too, that they could read him just like they all read Keith. "Sometimes you get too feminine," he'd fret, "or it just comes out." That's another reason Carlos would rather just hang out with the girls in the first place—he couldn't trust himself to act right.

And the stakes of screwing up were high. Once thrown off balance, Carlos often simply shut down altogether. "There was a time in my teens that I like closed myself off from the world completely," he explains. "I did not go out. I was not social with anyone. Just a simple thing like this"—he flicks his hand to and fro as though he's wiping away the space between us—"talking to someone, I would have an anxiety attack because I didn't know how to deal with it."

Those dark periods have recurred throughout Carlos's life. His world constricts around him as he literally loses his voice, often unable to speak at all, let alone leave the apartment and navigate the uncertainties of public space. "I couldn't even go to the store, I was so self-conscious and worried about what everybody thought." He sighs. "It's really hard. You know what to say, but your mind is like a complete blank. And that's when you worry. That's when you start sweating and anxiety comes—and all this other stuff, all this other baggage."

His parents tried to understand what was going on when he'd have these episodes, but he could offer them little help in deciphering his behavior. After all, it didn't make much sense to him, either. He knew the shutdowns had a lot to do with his shifting personalities and the haunting sexual pull those different faces masked. But he didn't have any words for all that. Which made it particularly difficult for his mom to understand when he dropped out of school after the tenth grade. "I mean, I wanted to go to school, I wanted to study," he haltingly offers, still struggling to explain what went wrong. "I just couldn't deal. I couldn't deal with the people and the fact that I was different."

. . .

At twenty-one, Carlos thought he'd finally found a solution to
the dissonance of his life. Although, at first, it involved yet another personality.

The game would start late at night, after everybody had gone
to bed. The apartment he and his parents shared could get like
Grand Central Station during the day, with friends and family
constantly coming and going and meddling and demanding his
attention. Not until the wee hours could he find a little space for
himself, and that's when he'd dial into the Internet and log in
to his favorite chat rooms to start exploring being homosexual.

Sitting in front of his computer screen in the quiet, otherwise dark apartment, Carlos felt safe, comforted by the presumed anonymity the medium provided. His computer mouse
would act like the gears of some enchanted transporter on
which he could dart in and around wholly new realms, exploring foreign ideas and experiences until he found ones that he
could make his own. But even in the distant, noncommittal
world of the Web, he wasn't prepared to reveal too much, not to
his interlocutors and not to himself. Plus, he didn't really know
anything about sites where gay men talk to each other openly.
So instead he logged in to straight chat rooms and posed as a
woman.

He'd develop elaborate identities and use them to seduce
men into sexy conversations, dangling the false possibility of an
in-person rendezvous to keep them engaged in the cybersex. It
was utterly thrilling. In these chat rooms, he could reverse the
roles of his real-life relationships, uncovering the secret sexual
fantasies held by the same sort of men from which he'd always
carefully hidden his own desires. He'd always been so skittish
around the men he knew, so frightened of saying or doing the
wrong thing and tipping them off to his homosexuality that he'd
steadfastly remained stiff and closed. As a result, he never developed meaningful enough relationships with other guys, even

his brothers, to really get inside their feelings and thoughts, to really learn what makes other guys—*normal* guys—tick. "I was afraid of men and would really not conversate, or relate to them in general," he explains. And he didn't know any other gay guys, that's for sure. "So, it was like no contact with men, at all." But online, all that could change. In his cybersex chats with the straight boys he seduced there, he both opened windows into their raw male arousal and dangerously indulged his own, all without taking any actual risks. "I'm just glad that I satisfied whatever needs they had," he cheekily quips. "I had a good time."

Doing cyberdrag as a straight girl also offered him a sort of training-wheels for his real sexuality. He explored what turned him on and how to talk about it, and began the slow, difficult process of emotionally owning those physical feelings. Modern gay politicos and community organizers often work tirelessly to downplay the *sexual* part of sexual politics and identity. It's an understandable reaction to the culture wars—to play up the similarities rather than the differences between gay and straight lives, in an effort to gain acceptance and equal rights even if they come without equal status. But the reality remains that, for most people coming out, it's their sexual wants and desires that separate them from their peers. With honest public discussion about those desires shunned, even the most politically and socially experienced gay folks can spend a lifetime sorting out how to genuinely own their libidos, and thus how to healthily and meaningfully incorporate them into their lives. Carlos surely had a long way to go in that process, but it's fitting that he began down the road in a hypersexual hetero space. He'd spent twenty-one years repressing his real thoughts and fantasies, and it took some greasing of rusted wheels and joints to get the sexual engine up and running. He used the officially sanctioned test-track of straight sex to do so.

But as he grew gradually more comfortable with the mechanics of his sexuality, at least online, he finally began to slowly branch out through the Web in search of gay-specific things. First he found gay porn, and then through the porn he found gay chat sites. Yahoo! hosts thousands of online "groups." On these electronic-messaging bulletin boards, organically generated by the portal's users, people swap messages about things ranging from building model airplanes to having extramarital affairs. There are thousands of groups for gay men alone, and Carlos liked to poke around in them. He was hanging around in one of the more popular gay male groups one night when he got a message.

>>Hey, remember me?
>>Um, no.

It was another Latino guy, from Orlando and a couple years older, and the guy was convinced he'd chatted with Carlos before; Carlos was equally convinced they'd never met. He'd been careful not to bookmark any sites or to inadvertently add any guys to the "buddy" list on the instant-messaging tool he had on the computer. He was being discreet about this Web business and thus covered his tracks pretty well, just to be sure there were no awkward moments when some other family member or friend tried to use the machine. So it was possible he'd forgotten who this guy was. But he assumed it was more likely this was just a lame pickup line, an excuse the guy was using to talk to him. And so be it. What's the difference? Web romances have been born of stranger things, he figured.

"Look," Carlos typed. "I'm not the guy that you thought. But we could still be friends. We could talk."

Ricky turned out to be way different from the other guys in the Men's Lounge group. He wasn't so focused on getting laid, for one thing. Most guys in there were always demanding that Carlos send a picture of himself, usually insisting it show off his body or his dick or some other overtly sexual thing. There was no way Carlos was gonna take a picture like that, let alone send one out to God knows who. Anyway, that's not what he logged in to Yahoo! for. If he was horny he could look at porn or go to one of the straight chat sites for cybersex. He came here to talk, and that's what Ricky wanted, too.

Carlos and Ricky were hardly unusual in turning to the Web to find a way out of the isolation of being young and gay. Talk to anyone working with gay youth—particularly those stranded in places disconnected from the gay mainstream, whether they're in rural cultural hinterlands or in walled-off urban enclaves such as East New York—and you'll hear words like *lifeline* used to describe the Web's role, not just for meeting and interacting with other gay youth, but for finding examples of healthy contexts in which they can live out their burgeoning sexualities and sexual identities. But this virtual space isn't one queer youth can take for granted, either. Teens, sex, and the Internet make for a volatile combination in today's culture wars. Politicians, activists, and media makers trip over one another in their race to alert parents to the dangers of an unregulated World Wide Web, and the censoring solutions they come up with are blunt tools: they are as likely to block off access to nonpornographic gay-related sites as they are to edit out smut.

In this instance, the gay teens are actually caught in the cross fire of a war they've got nothing to do with. The real juice in the Web-safety debate lies in ominous warnings of predatory adults lurking a click away—a subject so resonant it's been eyed as a potential savior for the newsmagazine shows that are being killed by reality TV's ratings grabbers. After its 2004 debut of "To Catch a Predator," *Dateline NBC* rode the feature—in which producers stalk chat rooms and lure adults into would-be hook-ups with minors—to the top of the network's primetime lineup. There's little substantive reason for these fears. According to the National Center for Missing and Exploited Children, more than

70 percent of child sex crimes are actually committed by a family member, not a stranger on the Net. Other studies have found that the relatively small number of kids who report getting unwanted sexual solicitations while online—whether from adults or other minors—is actually on the decline. A federally funded 2006 report, conducted by the Crimes against Children Research Center at the University of New Hampshire and purporting to make the case for how dangerous the Web can be, revealed a drop in youth who said they'd faced unwanted virtual come-ons, from 19 percent to 13 percent between 2000 and 2005.

But reality rarely interrupts adults' dark fantasies about childhood sexuality, so entrepreneurs and policymakers around the country have jumped in to save teens from their electronic selves. In 2000 Congress demanded that all schools and public libraries getting federal money put filtering software on their computers to weed out sites considered "obscene" by the given local community's standards. The courts later said the law couldn't apply to public libraries, but let it stand in schools. As the dispute over the law wended its way through the courts, gay-youth advocates and public health researchers took a look at the most-used Web-filtering software programs and found it censoring more than pornography. GLSEN, for instance, found its own Web site, as well as sites that talked about gay-straight alliance clubs, blocked in many school libraries. The problem was the word *gay* itself. A 2002 Kaiser Family Foundation investigation found that if you put the leading filters on their maximum-security settings, they weeded out 60 percent of the nonsexual sites with the word *gay* that researchers checked; when set at medium security, they blocked a quarter of the gay sites. Kaiser noted that three-quarters of all schools used Web filters as of 2002. The 2006 Crimes against Children sex-solicitation survey found that 55 percent of families had put censoring software on their home computers.

Carlos had of course dropped out of school long ago, and his family probably couldn't have afforded filtering software even if they'd known about it. So he dodged this particular landmine in his rambling journey toward self-awareness, and he used the Web to leap over the walls—real and imagined—of his East New York life into a cyber-relationship with Ricky that would eventually radically reshape his world.

As Carlos was making his first tentative steps forward with Ricky, Lionel's carefully constructed sexual masks were also starting to lose their fit.

Once Hermone moved into the house, her and Lionel's relationship took on a volatility befitting the passions they both proudly carried through life. They dated off and on, breaking up and trying again and breaking up and trying again, testing out periods of nonmonogamy and nontraditional relationship setups in an effort to find a formula that worked. In the end, they decided to just accept the obvious: that they made better best friends than anything else. That's one thing that never came into question for the two of them, though it could be terribly confusing for others. Their bond was a deep and spiritual one, and whether they were dating or not they freely expressed their affection for one another. They'd flit around the neighborhood holding hands and hugging and laughing and joking like a couple of young lovers who'd mistaken their gritty, urban surroundings for an idyllic pasture from some cheesy romance novel.

At first, all of that showy amore was at least in part a matter of expediency: it was just a lot easier for Hermone, as an attractive young woman, to be attached to a man as she made her way around her new environs. It cut down on the catcalling and whistling and assorted tacky come-ons that men in the city feel entitled to throw at good-looking women. Guys will hiss at women loud enough to be heard across the street—"Pssssst.

Hey shortie! Pssssst. Hey girl, why the long face?" They'll lean out of the windows of their gypsy cabs and call out judgments on the ass of a woman making her way down the sidewalk, reducing her to the role of livestock on an auction block, or stalk in behind her rattling off obscenities masquerading as compliments. The torrent can be unbearable, if not necessarily threatening, and implying that you're already taken is the lesser hassle to trying to constantly fight off or drown out the unwelcome celebrity.

But in the end, Hermone and Lionel clung so openly to each other because they just didn't know any other way to act. They were lovers, whether their attraction included an erotic bond or not. It didn't much matter how other people took it.

The relationship was probably made all the more confusing to onlookers by the fact that Hermone was so insistently queer. Even when they were still dating, Hermone went out of her way to explain her lesbian identity to neighbors. As she made her way up and down Crystal, doing work in the garden or just stopping in the bodegas and hanging out with the neighbors, she took any opportunity she could get to announce that she was a lesbian, that she dated women and saw no need to conceal or otherwise hedge around the fact. "I just thought it was important for me to be out there in the neighborhood in that way," she matter-of-factly explains. That posture drew her attention, both good and bad, and it was that attention that really got Lionel thinking about himself.

Hermone had been pressing him for a while, actually, probing around about what he really felt sexually and why he wouldn't be more proactive about those feelings. He'd always just been honest with her when she asked these questions. He knew he liked guys, he explained, but he was afraid to acknowledge it to himself or to anyone else. "I'm scared," he'd bluntly admit. And she'd always been understanding and supportive, nudging him forward without being pushy. But one day she broke it down in a way Lionel wasn't expecting and couldn't ignore. "I feel you on being scared," she told him. "But the extent to which you're out is the extent to which you're an ally to me. Your not being out jeopardizes my safety."

That blew Lionel away. He knew how brave Hermone had been about putting herself out there in the neighborhood. He knew making that choice must have been hard on her, and that it surely required her to throw herself into some pretty intense encounters, armed with nothing but faith in the fact that honesty and openness would win out. But Lionel had never considered that, as she did all of this, she was also fighting against his downward pull. She explained how homophobia and the struggle against it works: that there's strength in numbers on her side and that fear like his emboldens the homophobes on the other side; that the homophobic attacks and outbursts that her and other out gays absorb come because the culprits expect to proceed with impunity, an expectation born from the fact that so many would-be allies are hiding in the closet, scared. It was an eye-opening conversation for Lionel. He'd never considered the dynamic relationship between the easiness of his cowardice and the difficulty of Hermone's courage.

"This was someone I would die and kill for," he'd explain to me years later, staring off into space and shaking his head in continued awe at his own hypocrisy. "And I was like, 'Wow, I can say I'd die and kill for you, but it's like, can you walk it?' "

So he started needling himself on the topic. What are you really so scared of? he'd ask himself. And he couldn't escape the truth. "It was largely, just scared of myself, scared to be a faggot. And it was a lot of internalized shit. Because the actual physical shit—I mean, come on, I'm six foot two. I can carry myself pretty well." He knew he wasn't actually worried about getting attacked or beaten up. No, the problem was internal. And being scared of himself just wasn't something Lionel could sit with very long.

He didn't have many gay male friends at the time, but there was one guy he was close to and, truth be told, that he'd always felt something more than friendship for. He invited the guy over for dinner one night when everybody else was out and about, telling himself that they were just going to hang out as usual but knowing he had other motives in the back of his mind, and below his belt. "I used my friendship with him to get some," Lionel jokingly admits now.

They ate dinner and sat down on the couch to talk in the big, spacious front room of Lionel and Hermone's Crystal Street house, and before long it became clear that, as Lionel had hoped, his friend had ulterior motives, too. They made out and had sex and, predictably, "that turned into drama." Lionel enjoyed the experience, but it was too much too fast. "I freaked out," he plainly admits, throwing his hands up at an analysis too obviously accurate to dissemble about. "And I didn't call him for like five months, or some crazy shit."

It's not a reaction he's proud of, and it didn't sit well with him at the time either. The encounter nagged at him throughout those months of hiding out from his friend until, finally, he realized this had all been going on for far too long. Not just this business with his buddy, but his whole sexual charade—the random, sporadic episodes of "messing around with a dude"; his bizarre assertions, when pressed on the issue, that "everybody's homosexual" or "it's fluid." Those are the kind of prevaricating responses he'd given to the gay teens he'd encountered during the high school teaching gig he had before he moved to East New York. Somehow, all the gay kids in the school smelled him out. Maybe it was because of his politics, that he'd always made clear to students and administrators alike that, as he puts it, "I wasn't having any kind of homophobic mess in my classroom." His posture was just the opposite of the one so many gay high schoolers encounter. He not only refused to overlook even passing, coincidental antigay remarks, he also found ways to bring up gay people and to support the gay kids who were out. And they, in turn, were bold enough to ask why. Was he gay? "But they didn't ask the right question," he says now, laughing at his ability to split the finest of hairs. "If they would have just asked, 'Are you into dudes?' I might have said yes."

But after the talk with Hermone and the hookup with his friend, Lionel no longer appreciated such narrow distinctions. Slowly, he began testing out Hermone's approach, finding ways to casually toss a gay sexual identity into his interactions with newfound friends and colleagues in the neighborhood.

By this point, Lionel and his housemates had set up a series of organizing and community-building projects that aligned with their broader goals for using the house as a catalyst for change in the neighborhood. Each of them took charge of a piece that fit their skills and temperaments and ran with it, and all of the programs were really taking off. They had a media-training piece that one roommate ran in the basement, where young aspiring videographers learned and honed their art. They all worked on the community garden and found ways to organize people through it; Hermone held public yoga classes there when it was nice out, for instance. She also took on a range of both formal and informal healing projects—she worked at Rikers Island, the city's massive penal colony, leading a women's group; she counseled young Brooklyn women who'd had abortions, bringing to bear her own experience going through the emotionally taxing process.

Lionel took on organizing around housing instability in East New York, bringing homeowners together to figure out how to slow down the neighborhood's breakneck foreclosure rates and chase off predatory lenders. A neighborhood economic-development corporation got some temporary funding to deal with the issue, and they hired Lionel to run the program. The issue went beyond the houses themselves: with homes quickly turning over, whether by foreclosure or by families selling off to developers looking to flip the property, the constant churning of people stood in the way of broader community-building efforts. People couldn't put down deep enough roots to come together and take care of each other and their neighborhood. So it was Lionel's charge to round up homeowners and plug them into a grassroots movement for stability. He'd sit in the families' small, homey front rooms, presenting himself as the polite, respectful young man he is and carefully explaining why they had to band together and how they could do it.

"There's this group of people who are taking these developers on," he'd explain. "Now, these developers got a lot of money. They pay off most people, they buy people out. But we're building this crew. And the crew is tight right now. But we can get divided"—that was his opening, and having created it he'd then carefully back into coming out, using his sexual orientation as a straw man argument against counterproductive infighting— "like, such and such says, 'Oh, so and so is a womanizer.' Or, 'Lionel's a faggot.' And I'm gay, it's true." He'd pause just enough to let the disclosure sink in, but then keep moving along with his pitch for power in unity.

Nobody flinched. There was one couple who were the kind of evangelical Christians Lionel would have expected a backlash from. But even as they insisted every meeting open with prayer, they embraced Lionel as a son, never finding a conflict between his sexuality and their spirituality. "We built a strong core of like fifteen people who were like, 'It's all good. This is Lionel.' We built a real tight family."

And as Lionel and Hermone's house later morphed into the neighborhood's informal gay community center, the housing-activist group also welcomed the young queer kids Lionel brought around to help out making phone calls to drum up support. One woman—after meeting then fourteen-year-old Keith, who had moved from tormenting Carlos to hanging out on Crystal Street—discreetly pulled Lionel aside.

"He knows he's gay already?!" she gasped.

"Yeah, it's true," Lionel confirmed, frankly sharing his own awe at the kid's sexual awareness—which would of course have been an entirely unremarkable fact for Keith's straight peers. "Isn't it amazing? It took me like another twelve years!"

They laughed about it for a bit, and then the woman got to the real point: there was someone like Keith in her own family. "I need you to talk to my nephew, you know?"

This pull-aside maneuver became an increasingly familiar routine. Hermone in particular was a magnet for other women who were excited by her openness and eager to confide in her: You're gay? You should talk to my little cousin; So you're a lesbian? I'm gay too, actually, and I need help with my girlfriend. "There were all these 'baby dykes,' " Hermone jokes.

All of this led her and Lionel into the ever-popular gay parlor game of trying to guess who else in the neighborhood was "family," as the old gay euphemism goes—and Carlos was high on both of their lists. Lionel and Hermone would always laugh about it: Any time one of them walked by that newly erected, freshly scrubbed building over on Gary, they'd look up to find Carlos's window open and his stereo pumping out iconic gay tunes—Mariah Carey, Madonna, all variety of house-music mixes. Lionel had seen Carlos around the neighborhood a good bit, but the two hadn't really met. So he had no idea that Carlos hadn't come out to anybody in the world other than Ricky. Lionel just assumed from the way he carried himself that he was openly gay and, ironically, Lionel quietly drew strength from the fact. If this kid could be open about his sexuality in a neighborhood he's lived in his whole life, Lionel would think, why can't I? Still today, he thinks about Carlos when he needs a boost of courage for walking through the world as an openly gay man. "I think a lot of people don't know I'm gay," he explains. He knows his masculine, guy's-guy persona—no matter how much progressive, hippie edge he cuts it with—protects him from the assumptions that draw trouble for people like Julius and, he would presume, Carlos. And he admires their ability to step out every day anyway. "I have a lot of respect for that."

Carlos, meanwhile, was struggling to crank up the same respect for himself that Lionel projected onto him. He and Ricky's mutual longing for connection had sped their cyber-relationship along. Over the couple of months since they'd met, they'd chatted every night, started sending each other long e-mails, and eventually even started calling each other up and talking live every night too. The whole thing gave him a lot to think about.

"This was my first relationship," he recalls, still a little embarrassed about how green he was at the ripe old age of twenty-one. "I didn't really date." Not just men, but women either. He'd never even tried, figuring it'd be way too much for him to navigate a relationship with the sort of strong women he'd always known. "They know what they want," he laughs. "They don't play!"

As a result, just relating to Ricky as a lover, even from long distance, pushed him into exciting new realms. And he was doing pretty well with it, he thought. In fact, he was downright proud of the relationship and regularly bubbled over with excitement about their talks. He wanted to share all this joy with friends and family, and he found a way to do so by once again transposing the details of his on- and offline worlds: in a queered version of the girlfriend-in-Niagra-Falls adolescent cliché, he told everyone that he'd fallen for a gorgeous young woman who lived in Orlando. "I would be like, 'Oh, she's so pretty,'" he explains now, bashfully recounting his brazen lie, "but it was a man."

The specifics of the truth didn't matter to Carlos, though. The point was he'd fallen in love, and that was far too exciting a development in his life not to share it with his family. So what if he had to pervert the details in order to do so?

FIVE

Family's not an encumbrance for Julius, mainly because he's never really had any. He spent just about his whole life in foster homes before he came up to New York City, and he's been in one or another form of temporary shelter ever since his arrival here. But while he may not be able to relate to Carlos's caged-in feeling in East New York, he's equally mixed up about how to take charge of the wide-open life he's carved out for himself. Sitting in one of the sparse delis along Crystal Street, he tries explaining this to me, and to himself, but he's not finding the words. "I feel complacent," he begins awkwardly. "I can't, for some reason, do . . . *something*—with my schooling, with work." It's already late on a slow summer afternoon, so our food had been sitting all day in hot plates by the time we ordered it. We sit picking at our Styrofoam boxes of stale rice and overcooked chicken, sweating in the deli's thick, still air, and we can both feel the torpor pulling on Julius better than he can describe it. "I can't do anything other than just being in circumstances, just moving and struggling from one thing to another, one thing to another. I am *so* over it."

He's particularly discombobulated by sex, both by the years of sex work he's done and by his private exploits. Like everything else in Julius's life, sex has been an area of waxing and waning struggles to wrest control and self-determination—although, in this particular realm, the battle is waged not with some external force like his foster parents but with himself. Who drives his sexual decisions? Does he make choices or are they made for him? Or, more precisely, does he choose to have the terms dictated for him? And where does the sex end and the romance start? Or is it all the same thing?

By the time Julius moved to East New York, he was pretty well over trying to untangle these kinds of maddening and tiresome questions. Things had gone terribly wrong with his latest boyfriend, who he'd really thought it might work out with, and he'd found himself once again looking for a place to live, with no money. It'd been like that ever since he'd left north Florida at nineteen—a steady stream of relationship misfires and one failed effort after another at stabilizing his life.

He'd started at the infamous Covenant House, a Catholic Church–run organization that is the Wal-Mart of homeless youth services, here and around the country. Set up in 1972 in New York, Covenant House provides emergency shelter to tens of thousands of kids a year and holds enormous influence over both public- and private-sector efforts to deal with teen homelessness—a fact that greatly disturbs gay-youth-services providers. Covenant House insists it treats all the kids who come through its doors equally, but stories of mistreatment are legendary among homeless queer youth—transgender young women being forced to wear male clothes and to sleep alongside young men in gender-segregated quarters, often leading to rapes and other violent attacks; gay kids getting discharged when they complain to staff about harassment. During the years when Covenant House was the only resource around, gay youth regularly chose to simply sleep on the street rather than suffer the degradations and dangers they felt awaited them at the shelter. In part as a response to this fact, three gay-specific housing programs have grown up in the city. The largest of them, Green Chimneys, offers a range of housing services, from overnight emergency beds to independent-living setups for small groups of teens and young adults. The Ali Forney Center provides a similar range of services, and the gay-affirming Metropolitan Community Church's Sylvia's Place—named after legendary transgender activist Sylvia Rivera—offers overnight beds.

No concrete measure exists of how many gay youth are homeless, either nationally or locally. The New York City Council planned to attempt a real census in 2007, but the problem the city and others face in counting homeless youth of any kind is fundamental: How can they be identified? Simply counting the number of heads in a given area's youth shelters is a meaningless exercise, since by all accounts the number of kids without stable homes is far greater than the number who turn up in emergency housing. Some sleep on the streets, in places like Washington Square Park, where subway vents underneath park benches provide a warm, discreet place to curl up at night. But more often young people couch surf. This is particularly common among gay youth, who have either run away from or been chased out of their homes and stay temporarily with friends or extended family, tentatively making it by on the generosity of their hosts and moving on to the next couch or guest room when they wear out their welcome. These young people won't appear in any "homeless" census, but they are surely without homes. Their housing is entirely contingent on someone else's good will. Still others engage in what is known as "survival sex" —transactional hookups and relationships that neither the kid nor his or her companion would call prostitution, but which the young person gets into specifically for the purpose of finding a place to stay.

But despite these measurement difficulties, most people working in youth services today agree that lesbian, gay, bisexual, and transgender kids make up a far disproportionate share of young people without stable, safe housing. In a 2007 report exploring the dynamics of gay youth homelessness, the National

Gay and Lesbian Task Force, or NGLTF, culled several localized studies that, over the last two decades, have surveyed homeless youth and have pegged the share of them who are gay at anywhere from 3 to 50 percent. A 2005 survey in Chicago, for instance, declared roughly a quarter of the homeless youth who researchers identified there were gay. Another study, conducted by city officials in Seattle, found gay kids accounting for 40 percent of the city's homeless youth. Meanwhile, studies attempting to pinpoint the number of homeless youth overall have put the number anywhere between a low-end estimate of around 600,000 and a high end of 1.6 million, which was the number established in a 1998 U.S. Department of Housing and Urban Development report. If gay kids represent between 20 and 40 percent of these hordes, as NGLTF posits, then there are as many as 640,000 homeless gay youth in America.

By the time I met Julius, he'd been one of these statistics for three years, and he was tired. So when he landed in East New York, he was happy to give up his battle for control and accept whatever fate threw his way, to just have lots of casual sex, hang out in the West Village, and hit the clubs to dance into the wee hours of the morning. He led life passively, addressing each day for whatever it was worth, good or bad.

Sex itself had been confusing from the start, when he lost his virginity underneath a beach boardwalk to a nameless guy he met online. It was his senior year in high school and by that point he was already plotting his escape from Florida and the stifling life he had there with his foster parents. They lived along the Atlantic coast, just south of Jacksonville, in a tiny old conservative town, a place that was rich with history Julius felt he had nothing to do with and that was too small for him to get lost and explore a life of his own. For most of the time he lived there, he didn't give much thought to his sexual orientation. It was just not a subject that came up, at least not in any meaningful or relevant way, and anyway he was already clear about what he liked, even if he had no idea what that meant or what to do about it.

"I definitely liked boys, and I knew that from back, back, *back* in the day, honey. From when I was seven years old!" Julius is accelerating into the spitfire, take-no-prisoners speed at which he has his best conversations. He moves along at such a clip that his words fall behind, leading him to trail sentences off in a staccato series of placeholders—"da-da, da-da, da-da," he'll offer, unconcerned about whether listeners are able to keep up any better than his own mouth. "I wasn't butch or femme or anything," he explains of his high school mannerisms. "I mean, now I'm very femme, but back then I wasn't anything. But I'll tell you this much, the black people in school knew that I was gay—and they would tell you that. They would tell you, 'That nigger is a faggot!' The white people, I fit right perfect in with them—by manners, by attire"—he was an honor student, he explains, and tracked into largely white classes where he adopted the preppy, button-down style of the math geek he was—"so none of them questioned my sexuality at all. But Erica! I hated that girl, miss honey." Erica was one of the black kids, and she thought Julius a sellout, or at least something short of an appropriate black man. "She would spit at me. On my locker, she wrote, 'Loser.' "

This last memory sends him into a fit of girly giggles, though it's more of a guffaw than a blush at the idea of cowering before such harassment. These days, swishing around in East New York, the stakes of being an outsider are a lot higher. It's not just his imagination: the young toughs who run what remains of the neighborhood drug trade give him constant shit. They shout taunts of faggot this and punk-ass that; if he mouths off they threaten him with the sort of violence he knows they're capable of. There've been too many incidents for him to dismiss their threats as idle boasts. He knows young black gay people get killed and terrorized in Brooklyn with disturbing ease and regularity.

Like nineteen-year-old Rashawn Brazell, whose dismembered body the cops found scattered around Brooklyn in February 2005, his limbs shoved into a plastic bag and tossed onto the subway tracks in Bed-Stuy, his torso similarly deposited in a recycling plant near the East River waterfront. Police posters offering rewards for information about Brazell's murder still hang on poles in central Brooklyn subway stations, his boyish brown face staring out from an increasingly iconic family photo emblazoned onto the worn bills. By all accounts, two years later cops still remained entirely in the dark about what happened to the teen, who had last been seen leaving his home on Valentine's Day. His severed head was never found.

Brazell's case has come to symbolize the palpable sense of potential violence many young gay, lesbian, bisexual, and transgender people of color feel in the city. But his was just the most shocking of several recent attacks. There's twenty-seven-year-old Dwan Prince, for instance, who guys just like the ones who taunt Julius beat into a coma in June 2005. When he testified at the 2006 trial of the one person charged in the attack, Prince was still paralyzed on the left side of his body and face despite three surgeries. He said the last thing he remembers is saying goodbye to his brother at a central Brooklyn bus stop. Two witnesses saw Prince getting stomped and kicked for five minutes by three men, one of whom warned the witnesses, "Leave it alone, son, the nigger's a faggot," according to *Gay City News*. The twenty-three-year-old young man who was later convicted in the beating said the attack started because Prince flirted with him, explaining that Prince "came at me wrong."

The violence isn't confined to Brooklyn, either. In 2003 Sakia Gunn, a fifteen-year-old lesbian, was stabbed to death after rebuffing a man's come-ons while waiting for a bus in Newark, New Jersey. She and her friends were making their way home from a night hanging out in the West Village when the killer began aggressively flirting with one of them; Gunn told the guy they were lesbians and he attacked. In 2006, one of the city's most famous drag performers, Kevin Aviance, was beaten so badly outside of an East Village gay bar by a group of fellow black men that his jaw had to be wired shut. In May 2005, thirty-two-year-old Kenmoore Thomas was beaten to death with a barbell in his Harlem apartment; neighbors, who alerted the police, heard Thomas's body pounding on the floor for ten minutes as the attacker smashed his face.

Cops believe Thomas was killed in what is known as a "pickup" crime, in which a would-be sexual encounter goes awry. Often, as was the case in the widely publicized 1998 murder of white college student Matthew Shepard, gay men are targeted by criminals who lure them into supposed encounters and then, rather than just robbing them, commit acts of graphic violence. Michael Sandy, a twenty-nine-year-old black man from Brooklyn, was the latest such victim in New York City. In October 2006, he met a group of white young men on Adam4Adam and rendezvoused with them at a park near one of Brooklyn's beach neighborhoods. They attacked him and chased him onto a highway where he was hit by a car and killed. Each year, anti-gay watchdogs chronicle as many as a dozen of these and other murders around the country, though few get the attention of Shepard's. "I think we all can acknowledge that in a lot of ways, for a lot of people, Matthew Shepard did represent this kind of idealized victim," New York City Anti-Violence Project director Clarence Patton told *Gay City News* following Sandy's murder, which like Brazell's and Gunn's and Thomas's garnered only passing local media coverage. "He was young, he was white. He was not in one of the kind of classic gay ghetto, urban areas."

Julius has never faced this sort of brutal violence, but when he lived up in Harlem he got jumped in his own apartment building by someone who targeted him for robbery because he was gay and thus presumed to be weak. Here in East New York, guys who Lionel is butch enough to dismiss as "little wannabe gangsta badasses" and not flinch at leave Julius terrified as they huff and puff and scowl at him every time he passes by. The misplaced "Oreo cookie" insults of kids like his high school nemesis Erica are quaint memories by comparison, something he can laugh at nostalgically. "Oh miss honey, I couldn't stand it," he says, smirking and shrugging at the threat Erica and her friends seemed to present at the time. "In my mind, they were envious, jealous haters."

Meanwhile, he harbored a series of what would have been—gender and race aside—just typical teen crushes on the white boys in his Advanced Placement classes. Like Val, whom he worked alongside doing landscaping the summer before senior year. They'd be painting or raking leaves or cutting grass and Val, known as something of a player because of his classic good looks, would stay shirtless too often for Julius's comfort. He was cute in the clean-cut way people there valued, with blond highlights and bright blue eyes staring out over a strong, angular chin he kept smoothly clean-shaven, if a bit pimply. He never seemed to mind Julius's obvious stares at his naked torso, but as they worked he'd prattle on and on about the girls he liked at school—who was the prettiest and whom he'd like to do this with and which one he'd like to do that with. By the end of the summer Julius really couldn't stand the guy.

One day after the school year started back up, Val and Julius's American studies teacher gave out a quirky assignment, asking each student to write a poem about himself or herself that they'd then read to the class. Julius doesn't remember everything in Val's poem, but he recalls how it captivated everybody. It was gripping and honest, revealing in just the way that the assignment was meant to be, and at the end Val dropped his bombshell: he was bisexual. It was 2001, and by that point in American life there were schools and towns where such an admission may not have meant that much, but Julius's was not one of them. "Gay, lesbian—it's not even a word you *use*," Julius explains, "unless you read about it in a newspaper: some gay guy got raped or bashed somewhere in a public stall."

Julius wasn't clear on why Val's coming out enraged him, but it did, and henceforth he didn't want the boy anywhere near him.

At the time, their American studies teacher had them engaged in yet another innovative assignment, designed to teach them about the world of financial management. The students all had to put together a stock portfolio and manage it on Yahoo! week to week over the course of the school year; Julius chose military contractors. He was sitting at the classroom computer checking out his stocks one day not long after the dramatic poetry reading, when Val walked up, the casual confidence that helped make him so attractive in full bloom.

"Hey, I need to use the computer."

"Yeah, OK."

Julius never looked up, but instead worked hard to make his posture as curt and dismissive as his words, all of which was meant to quickly shoo Val away. But Val didn't leave. He just stood there looming in open violation of Julius's new unspoken rule that the two keep their distance.

"Yo, I'll call you when I finish," Julius snapped.

"No," Val fired back, now taunting and in deliberate provocation. "I'm ready for the computer."

"Go away. I'll call you when I'm done."

Val smirked and, empowered by his own newfound honesty, hit Julius where he knew it would hurt. "Oh I know that you want me, Julius."

He'd landed the blow he sought.

"Whatever, faggot!" Julius erupted.

A homophobic barrage followed as Julius dragged up every antigay slur he'd ever heard and flung them at Val with abandon—all for naught, since Val merely laughed and took the verbal punches with the same suave arrogance he'd used while talking about his would-be heterosexual conquests all summer. They each got tossed out of class, but in the end Val got most of the blame for the fight, which they both knew was only because school officials were not so comfortable with Val's new openness. It was a fine line between proud and brazen, as far as they were concerned, and Julius played on that sentiment by implying Val had made him uncomfortable. Which was true, if not for the stated reasons.

It didn't matter to Val, though. The incident simply confirmed for him that he had Julius's number, and as a result he didn't let up the rest of the school year. It was one baiting comment after another, any chance to call Julius out on his studied asexuality. And Julius knew it too. He ultimately credits Val's antagonistic antics with nudging him toward acting on his own feelings, in part because, in spite of their feud, Julius's plain desire for the guy never subsided.

One of the many extracurricular activities that kept Julius gratefully out of his foster family's home that senior year was working on the yearbook. He'd find himself alone in the yearbook club's workspace after school, thumbing through pictures of Val and poking around in AOL chat rooms. That's where he finally connected all the dots—his disinterest in girls, his lust for boys, and the fact that there were outlets for his desires even right there in north Florida. He had been playing around in the AOL chat rooms for about a month when he randomly decided to act on his fantasies.

One afternoon, in the slim hours between when he left school and when he went off to work, he was on his foster brother's computer talking to a guy—whose name he doesn't remember, or may just have never known—from a town about an hour's drive away. The guy had sent him some pictures, the sort of explicit stuff he'd quickly learned how to solicit from his fellow chatters, and the naked portrait stared out at him from his computer screen: a tallish white dude in his twenties with dark hair and a deep, caramelized beach-bum tan. Why not? he thought. There was nothing special about the guy, nothing that distinguished this day or this chat from any of the others he'd had over the last few weeks, but the guy was willing to drive all the way over to the beach by Julius's house. So why not give it a shot? Julius gave him directions.

He waited an hour and then walked out onto the narrow, scenic highway that ran up the coast, separating the water-front housing developments from the plots of public beach that the town had parceled out and numbered off. Julius had taken the short stroll up to the section he'd chosen for his date often enough to do it on autopilot, so there was nothing other than the still-bright late-afternoon sun to distract him, and as he walked he got scared. It wasn't so much that he was worried about meeting a stranger in a deserted beach parking lot, it was more that he wasn't sure exactly what the guy would expect of him. Was he gonna have to fuck the guy? Or would the guy want to fuck him? But he figured it was too late to worry about all that; he'd have to play it by ear.

When he got to the parking lot the man was waiting, leaning against his Toyota Corolla, looking a bit chubbier and a bit older than the photos he'd e-mailed. They climbed into the car anyway and the guy started making small talk. How old are you, he asked, because Julius's round, baby face—both boyish and masculine at the same time, resembling a young Nelson Mandela—made him look a good bit younger than his eighteen years. And the guy bizarrely wanted to talk about sexual identity, as well. Did Julius consider himself gay, or was he bisexual, even straight? But Julius couldn't have been less interested in any of this stuff. He was already nervous and the chitchat wasn't helping. To make matters worse, he could see the sun inching downward, which meant he didn't have much time before people would start getting home and wondering where he'd gone off to. Let's get to it, he thought.

"I have to be home. So how can we do this?"

They got out of the car and walked toward the beach. A line of dunes separated the parking lot from the sand, and a boardwalk stretched over the mounds to bridge the two territories. They clambered underneath the walkway and down into the dunes, putting them just out of sight in both directions. It was around seven o'clock, so most of the beach had emptied, but as they situated themselves Julius noticed a handful of people still swimming and fishing, and even once the two were out of sight the knowledge of their neighbors made Julius still more tense. The tension in turn made him all the more blunt and transactional about the encounter.

"I've never been fucked before."

"Um, so you must be really tight then?"

"I guess so. I don't know. I've never done it. I'll give you a blow job."

This wasn't going well. All Julius's online bravery had drained out, and the guy wasn't doing much to conceal his obvious discomfort either. Instead, he just pulled down his pants and wrapped the beach towel he'd brought from the car around his naked waist.

"No, you fuck me."

He handed Julius a condom and some lubricant. Julius never even took his pants all the way down, just opened them enough to put on the rubber and do the deed. They didn't kiss, barely even touched, and when it was over the man pulled up his pants and abruptly left. Julius took off the condom and, rather than throwing it down there, climbed back out of the dunes and made his way to the bathrooms by the parking lot. He rushed inside, went to the stalls, and flushed the condom down the toilet. "I washed my hands, I went home, took a shower—and I was done."

He wasn't done playing online, but he was at least temporarily done meeting people. Someone he chatted with told him about a cruisy public bathroom, and occasionally he'd ride his bike by the spot, but he never stopped. All that seemed way too sketchy to him after the beach experience, and all the guys were these older, hippie-looking white dudes anyway. He wasn't interested in that, so he just let the idea of acting on his sexual desires go—he'd never even considered what it would mean to act on the emotional ones. Instead, he began to plot his escape altogether, because he was also done with north Florida. He'd never been to New York City, but he'd heard all about it—a place packed with black people, gay people, immigrants; a big messy jumble in which he could be whatever he wanted to be. He set his sights northward.

Julius didn't have much to leave behind in Florida, either emotionally or materially. His foster home was a disturbingly upside-down universe, and one that would eventually end up the subject of a criminal complaint from Julius and the other young men and boys who lived there. His foster mother and her mid-twenties biological son, both of whom were white, were movers and shakers in their town—small-business owners known as civic-minded, hardworking entrepreneurs. They owned a bakery, a flight school, and assorted other enterprises. They were heavily involved in not just their own church, but others around the region. And they had a foundation that was nominally dedicated to helping disadvantaged youth—a half-dozen of whom lived with them as foster kids. But Julius charges in an affidavit filed with the local sheriff's office and the FBI that the foundation was a sham. He says the mother and son forced him and the other kids living there to sign made-up sob-story letters asking churches for donations to help support the needy kids, to give them new opportunities and experiences. But then the youth were also each forced to hold several jobs—Julius's day started at two in the morning with a one-thousand-person paper route before school; in the evenings and on weekends he had a dishwashing and line-cooking gig at a nearby restaurant; summers included a day job—and they had to turn over all of the money they earned to the fake foundation. When they weren't working for pay, they were doing manual labor at the family's various properties, or touring churches in the region to do in-person fundraising. Any resistance the kids showed to being cash cows for the mother and her son was met with both physical and psychological brutality, Julius charges; he was regularly forced to sleep out in the garden toolshed for being impudent, and he actually came to enjoy the space for the peaceful respite it offered from the stress and chaos inside the house. The foster mother, for instance, regularly called the boys niggers and made offhand remarks about how ignorant the blacks they encountered were.

All of the foster children found different ways of coping with this trauma. During the four years he lived there, Julius's mechanism was to retreat into his school studies and extracurriculars, activities his foster mother had to allow in order to keep up appearances. So as he plotted his escape, his first thought was college.

As graduation approached, he applied to a bevy of Florida schools; one small local college even offered him a partial scholarship. But working out all the financing was going to involve jumping through a lot of administrative hoops—machinations that ultimately required the active participation of his foster mother, who was not only uninterested in helping but eager to keep him dependent on her dubious charity. School clearly wasn't going to be his way out—or if it was, it was going to take time and patience, a resource he didn't feel like he could afford any longer. He was going to need a far more blunt tool, something that would shatter his ties to the family altogether. "I said, 'I wanna leave.'" Which raised an obvious question. "OK, so how you gonna leave?"

First he came up with a list of cities he could flee to. There was Miami, but that was too close for him, if his foster mom really wanted to she could probably hunt him down there and find a way to bring him back. Los Angeles was attractive, but it seemed to present fairly insurmountable logistical challenges. New York City, however, was just one long bus ride away and, more importantly, it was the city that he figured had the most of what he direly wanted in the new life he was going to build: "I knew there was gay life in New York."

So he got online and started trying to figure out what the city had to offer. It was a tedious process, because he knew he had to be careful. He'd already been busted once at school for getting on gay chat sites. In addition to his yearbook-club computer exploits, during lunch period he'd sneak off and sequester himself in the library to play online canasta and hide out from all the pressures of the bustling cafeteria. Things were too wide open there, too many of the school's different social strata collided for him to comfortably navigate it all. No, if he couldn't be in his smart-kids' bubble, he preferred the solitude of the library's computer games and, after the whole Val thing, occasionally some chat. But one day the librarian pulled him aside and told him he'd been leaving an electronic trail of crumbs. She'd been sweet about it, more supportive than scolding, and even showed him how the tracking software worked and how, if he was going to do this at home and didn't want anyone to know, he should at least delete the "cookies." He was thankful for her generosity, because the whole episode had been sloppy and he knew he couldn't afford to make the same mistake at home. If anybody in his foster family found out what he was up to there'd be hell to pay, and they'd ruin his plans by watching him like a hawk. So after each furtive research session, Julius went back and erased all the electronic footprints in the computer's memory. It slowed the process down quite a bit, but better safe than sorry.

"I looked up a lot of stuff, miss honey. I looked up shelters.

I looked up resources. Gay places." He found the gay community center in the Village and the YES program. He found Covenant House and two other homeless youth shelters, which led to still more resources and services to help young people, gay and straight. And armed with this information, he sketched out a plan. "All I needed was $120. That bought a ticket from Florida to New York on Greyhound."

Julius's deftness in finding what he needs online is just the sort of skill people like George Ayala say adults who want to help young gay people are failing to exploit. Ayala has spent years working in HIV-prevention and harm-reduction programs aimed at gay men of color. He ran the Institute for Gay Men's Health, a unique partnership between Gay Men's Health Crisis in New York and AIDS Project Los Angeles that publishes a series of monographs, journals, and essay collections in which gay and bisexual men of color talk candidly about their sexual and emotional lives. Ayala, a Latino gay man, is a soft-spoken, seemingly reserved presence in the prevention world. But his words and ideas, no matter how evenly delivered, regularly break industry taboos, challenging the too often simplistic formulas for "intervening" to mitigate "risk" in gay men's lives. He's a particularly harsh critic of one-dimensional approaches to prevention, whether they be the just-wear-a-condom mantra or the recycled effort to reduce risk by playing on men's fears of HIV and other ills. "We need to figure out ways to present information that's not out of context," he explains. "We really think about risk in ways that are disconnected from people's lives."

The Web, he says, is an ideal example. The anxieties the broader public has about young people and the Internet have found their way into the gay community as well, and well-meaning folks from public health officials to community leaders have begun to fret over the damage people like Julius can do to themselves there. "For me, I see it as an opportunity," Ayala counters. "I think of the Web as a communication mechanism." So while at the Institute for Gay Men's Health, he and his colleagues built a Web site (which is no longer available) that helped young gay men game out choices around dating, sex, and drugs. Tricked out with house music and stylized cartoon characters, the site invited visitors to travel through a set of virtual scenarios in their social lives. You'd head out for a night clubbing or log in to a chat room and would be presented with a series of choices along the way. Each choice led to a new scenario until you eventually arrived at a consequence: You've made it to the club and you're on the dance floor enjoying yourself, but you've taken a given party drug. What happens if you pass up a drink of water enough times? You get dehydrated to the point of needing medical attention. You meet a guy online who wants to hook up. How do you bring up condoms and STDs with him? In this sense, the Web offers a unique opportunity to introduce someone like Julius to a thought process he had no other way of encountering. Rather than railing about potential dangers lurking online for Julius, Ayala argues, we need to spend more time planting these sorts of compelling, educational devices for him to stumble upon while clicking around.

Having developed his escape plan, Julius bided his time over the summer after graduation, squirreling away as much money as he could from his restaurant job by telling his foster mom that his pay had been cut, and not quite fully giving up on the chance that financing for college would work out. He even put in an application at Borough of Manhattan Community College in New York. And he reached out to his high school guidance counselor.

Julius and the counselor, Stevie, had become close over the course of his senior year as he began sharing details of his home life with her and explaining how the situation had frustrated his ambitions for higher education. He trusted Stevie because her son Jamie, whom he met in the Advanced Placement classes, was one of a handful of kids Julius could really consider a friend. Stevie and her husband, Dan, were as close to progressive as you'd likely find in a small, conservative southern town, and they engaged their son's life in a personal, hands-on way. They were the kind of parents that encouraged Jamie's friends to call them by their first names. And when they heard Julius's stories about his foster family's behind-the-scenes deviousness they were outraged. They didn't know exactly what to make of it all, but they knew Julius had always been a focused, reliable student; that despite his clearly difficult background he'd harnessed an enthusiasm rarely seen in even the most privileged kids. So they trusted him when he said he had to get out of there, and that he had a plan that would enable him not only to break out but to go to college and continue the impressive development they'd witnessed so far. They wanted to know how they could help. And that's where the New York community college application paid off for Julius.

All summer, either Dan or Stevie would drop by the slightly upscale restaurant where Julius worked to buy him lunch and talk him through his crisis. How were things holding up at home? What was his long-term plan if he did in fact leave town? Where did things stand with all of his college applications? He'd been accepted up in New York, he explained, but he had to figure out how to get there, how to get established and find a job so he could pull it off. That's how they could help, he said. They could cosign a loan to pay off the college tuition and living expenses. It was only a partial lie. He'd actually applied to the community college much too late in the year to get in for the fall semester, but he'd been lobbying the college and at least one administrator had in fact said the school might be able to work out a late admission. Julius figured he could get up there and talk to these people in person, make it all work somehow. He just needed the start-up money. Dan and Stevie, who had worked in New York in her younger years, thought the plan made sense.

After all, the city had lots of resources available to young folks that could help Julius if the plan went awry; if he was going to run off someplace and start off on his own, New York was probably the best place for him, she figured. So they agreed to help with the loan when it got to the time and to support him however they could in getting to New York, and they offered up their home as a safe haven for him if things got too out of hand with his foster family in the interim.

So one afternoon in September 2002, Julius waited until the house was empty and hurriedly packed up his things—two bags of clothes, a few books, some papers and journals, an alarm clock, his posters and his CDs. He also stole some diamond earrings and $300 in cash from his foster mother's bedroom. He rang up Dan and Stevie, and Dan sped over to pick him up. Two days later, he and Dan drove out to the nearest Greyhound station.

Dan and Stevie offered him what help they could for the journey itself. Dan gave him $500 and bought him a ticket for the afternoon bus; Stevie fixed up enough food to get him through the twenty-two-hour journey—some sandwiches, fried chicken, a big jug of lemonade, fruit, a batch of cookies. "It was very Down South," he laughs now, full of affection for the couple, who would become his surrogate, long-distance parents during his tumultuous years bouncing around on New York City's streets. "Dan gives me the man talk. He tells me, 'You're grown now. You've been to high school, now you're a man. Use this money well. Don't get into shit like some people get into in New York.' He told me about the crime. Be strong. Da-da, da-da . . .'" And at three o'clock, Julius got in line and climbed onboard what he figured would be a bus to freedom.

He scoffs at the memory: "They call it express, but it has many stops." He settled into a seat in the middle—to avoid the "crackheads" piled into the back rows—and dug into his journal, scribbling out a letter to his foster family that he'd never actually send. He was nineteen now, he informed them, and they had no real claim on him, so he was off to start his new life. Don't come looking. And as he wrote he slowly migrated up I-95 toward urbanity, passing through Jacksonville, where hordes of other black folks packed in and filled up every bit of spare space; then through Savannah, Georgia, where he'd once visited a church with his foster mom and sung in the choir; then a drive straight through the night to Fayetteville, North Carolina; on up to Philly; through New Jersey's Penn Station, and finally, down into the Lincoln Tunnel that connects the island of Manhattan to the mainland.

To someone who has never been to New York City, as Julius had not, emerging through the Manhattan side of the tunnel can feel like exploding into an altogether different universe. The long narrow passage opens suddenly onto the city's famously chaotic web of activity. You wind along an off-ramp in a snaking line of cars crammed bumper to bumper and laying incessantly on their horns; that dead-ends into the far western edge of Times Square, with pedestrians scurrying around in between any spaces the vehicles fail to fill, the skyline chockablock with flashing neon and giant rotating billboards; the monstrously gray Port Authority Bus Terminal hovers like the Death Star over the whole scene. It inspires one of two reactions: utter revulsion or, as in Julius's case, sheer thrill. "I was fucking excited! And the first thing I saw? When the bus was pulling into Port Authority: Covenant House, which was right there. And there was the kids outside. I mean *flamboyant* kids!"

He was home, he thought, free to start completely over and shape his life as he chose. He'd check into Covenant House eventually, he figured. But it'd been a long trip, and as exciting as all of this was it was also pretty overwhelming. He needed to catch his breath and get his footing before diving in, and he had a meeting at the college on Monday morning that he wanted to be fresh and rested for. With $800 in his pocket and diamonds he figured to be worth at least a few thousand bucks in a pawn-shop, he could afford to start off in a nice hotel. He had it like that, right? No sweat. It took some roaming to find the right place, but he finally came across the hundred-year-old, elegant Gershwin Hotel, right in the center of midtown Manhattan. "I was like, I'm gonna survive in New York City!"

SIX

For all the pain Julius's survival in New York City has cost him, one place where he has found the payoff he sought when plotting his escape from north Florida is the West Village, where night after night throngs of black and Latino queer youth gather on a pier that stretches off the end of Christopher Street into the Hudson River. Every evening, particularly in summer but to be certain year-round, the largely teenage crowd converges by the dozens from all over the tristate area. If Prospect Park is the space claimed by gay youth of color in Brooklyn, the Christopher Street pier is their fingerhold on the city at large. They come from disparate places as far flung as the South Bronx and Newark, New Jersey, in search of a place where, put simply, they belong.

Christopher Street stands as one of America's great gay landmarks. The latest incarnation of the Stonewall bar sits at the street's far eastern end. The original tavern, a mafia-run stink hole that has no actual relationship to today's namesake, was the site of the 1969 uprising that's widely considered the dawn of the American gay rights movement. During a routine police shakedown of the bar in June of that year, a number of the patrons who frequented it suddenly decided that, on that night, they would not go quietly into the paddy wagon. Five days of unrest unfolded and a movement was born. Because of that historical happenstance, Christopher Street and the surrounding western Greenwich Village neighborhood became the city's first and still most popularly known gay enclave. Gay communities worldwide commemorate the event with pride festivals and parades held every June.

The uprising, which has since been christened the Stonewall Rebellion, was primarily fueled by a gaggle of homeless gay teenagers, a mélange of white, black, and brown migrants who'd been chased out of or fled from their families and had taken residence in tiny Sheridan Square park, across the street from Stonewall. Bob Kohler, who was among those who founded the Gay Liberation Front in the days following the Stonewall riots, lived nearby at the time and befriended the young people. He still lives in the Village and volunteers at a youth program serving today's "pier kids." "It's just different names and different faces. They come from the same places, basically—here, there, and everywhere. Very little difference," says Kohler, a tall, handsome white guy who grew up in the city and who, in his forties at the time of the Stonewall Rebellion, was even then a rare adult ally. "We in the general population, gay or straight, were not really aware of these kids until Stonewall."

But by that time the kids had long since staked claim to both Sheridan Square and the Christopher Street pier. The West Village has a long and often sordid history, but it became a place where men cruised for both private and commercial gay sex in the late 1950s, after the shipping industry waned and left the West Side piers abandoned. The homeless kids—universally male in Kohler's memory but also primarily the sort of gender-bending personalities that would today be called transgender—shuttled between their makeshift homes on Sheridan Square's park benches and the vacant, cavernous warehouses on the piers, selling sex to closeted men. "They were a bunch of broken-down old piers where anything went. And the kids used to hustle down there. Cars used to come over from New Jersey at night, mostly married men, and the kids used to get two bucks for a blow job, depending on what they looked like. I think the most any of them ever made was five bucks—they wouldn't tell you that," he jokes, "but I think that was about the tops. And it was a hard life doing it, because the cops would pick them up. And if they didn't beat them up, the cops would take them down into an alley and make them blow them. Things like that."

Kohler recognizes that this scene was hardly safe and welcoming, that it was a strange launching pad from which to ignite a movement. "But it was ours," he explains. He leans forward in his chair and points out of the big windows that line the far wall of his colorful railroad apartment, perched above the same streets he and those kids demonstrated in decades ago. "We had to claim a space," he says, now in his eighties but still urgent and insistent about the need. "As far as Gay Liberation Front went, we didn't give a fuck about straight people; we were there to make it better for gays." That meant starting from the beginning. "We didn't have anything, but the main thing we didn't have was space." So in the wake of the kids' spontaneous uprising, Kohler and his colleagues fanned the flames of their passions. Among other tactics, they staged a "stoop-in," having gay people camp out along Christopher Street's stoops and sidewalks. "In our arrogance, we said Christopher Street is the gay street. That's it—never mind any of the people who *lived* all along Christopher Street," he jokes. "And that spread like wildfire. It was like somebody waved a magic wand. People came from all over."

The spell hasn't been broken over generations of queers, but it has enchanted different sectors within the gay community, from the leathermen and Village People–style butch "clones" of the 1970s to the often-touristic scene of more recent years. Walk down Christopher Street after dark nowadays, though, and you may think you've stumbled onto the grounds of a high school campus populated entirely by black and brown queer kids. The chaotic, vibrant scene far more closely resembles the counter-cultural ethos of Kohler's early gay liberation than today's more subdued gay mainstream. People make statements with their bodies—big, bold, outsize declarations of their existence. Experimentation in style is rewarded, creating a world more like a Michael Jackson video than the Abercrombie & Fitch catalogs pantomimed in many gay spaces. Young men in various stages of gender subversion similarly overshadow the modern gay cult of masculinity. They show off colorful head rags; looping, bejeweled belts; snug, low-rise jeans that would make Britney Spears blush. It's the most transgender friendly space in the city, where young men and women shape and reshape their gender identities with a comfortable fluidity. You're more likely to see "butch dykes" and "doms" sporting the hip-hop uniform of baggy jerseys and oversize jeans than dainty girls tiptoeing along on heels. And anyway, nobody tiptoes down Christopher Street—you swing and strut, arms locked around the waists of your friends and lovers. Or, in the vernacular, you "kiki" with your posse, "throw shade" at the doofs who don't get your style, and generally do your best to earn that highest of compliments—that whatever you got going on is just *fierce*.

The vast majority of the young people who hang out down here aren't old enough to get into the bars and clubs. So they primarily mill around and wind their way through Greenwich Village's maze of narrow streets, the Christopher Street pier serving as an anchoring base of operations as people come and go. There, on a tiny sliver of once-abandoned real estate poking off the end of Manhattan, they stake their own claim to space. For many, the pier is the closest thing they have to a home. For others, it's the only home where they feel fully welcomed, in all their queerness and all their blackness.

But none of that makes this space a necessarily secure one today. Nearly four decades after the original pier kids' rebellion, Julius and his friends' hold on Christopher Street and the pier is tenuous, challenged by area residents, the city's waterfront beautification plans, and the cops who back up both claims. In 2001 the city began gradually shutting down the West Side piers in order to rebuild them as an idyllic waterfront park to enhance an increasingly high-rent West Village. As the renewal project slowly closed off access to the piers, it drove the kids who hung out there into the surrounding residential streets and set up a bitter battle with homeowners. And when the space reopened in 2004, the "broken-down old piers" that generations of gays had adopted as home—many literally, even setting up make-shift shacks at one point—had been replaced by a lush lawn for sunbathers, canopied seating for picnickers, and a freshly paved bike path. Cops made it clear right away who was and was not welcome by aggressively enforcing a ban on late-night hanging out there and strictly policing the clean new restrooms, arresting transgender youth who tried to enter ones that didn't match the sex they were assigned at birth. But as today's pier kids struggle to defend their nearly forty-year-old squatting rights, they're still fighting for a dangerous sort of freedom, one that is born from the abandonment of Kohler's era as much as it is from liberation, and thus one that gives them equal room to build themselves up and tear themselves down.

Manny has never really understood all the fuss about the Christopher Street pier. He's been a couple times before and it's been fun enough, sure. But it never quite measures up to the mythic status Jason and others afford it. Maybe that's because it's always been just a jump-off spot for their nights out, a place to meet up with the rest of their crew before heading off to sneak into clubs. Tonight, however, looks to be different. The pier is the final stop in a day that hasn't involved much of anything beyond waiting around for the night to come. Things have devolved at school since Manny's initial flash of initiative at the start of ninth grade, and now, toward the end of that academic year, he's making it to class only sporadically. He's not even making it up to Trump Tower these days, actually; he and Jason are mainly just hanging around doing a whole lot of nothing, wallowing in the very inertia that's been driving him to spend time at the gay community center with his white friends from school. The tedium gets interrupted every couple of weeks for a big night out at whatever gay club they can sneak into, usually the eighteen-and-over night at Kurfew, a party for college students. But tonight's diversion promises to be something special. For weeks, everyone's been abuzz about this dance showdown to take place out on the pier.

So he and Jason train in from Brooklyn and make their way down Christopher Street to the giant four-lane highway that runs up Manhattan's western edge, separating the Village from the West Side piers. They join the crowd picking its way across the divide, hopping through speeding cars like characters in an early-generation video game. Once on the other side, they're greeted by a soundwave of house music pouring out of boom boxes, a rapid, driving beat that promises to push the party's energy upward. The city's waterfront-redevelopment plan is already under way. And that means the pier is gradually being reduced to a construction site, with a giant chain-link fence and temporary walls closing off broad swaths where young folks once gathered. It lends the scene a hardscrabble, illicit look that appeals to Manny's sense of public outlaw—it's clear they don't belong in this spot, and the prohibition makes their ostentatious presence exciting. Plus, the construction forces the crowd to cram into a still-smaller space, which amps up the excitement even further.

But as Manny strolls into this scene, he's gripped by something more than its urban-grunge setting and electric vibe. For him, there's also the totally unfamiliar tingle of kinship. It's spring of ninth grade and he's been going to the gay community center program for months now, and his queer identity is blooming, certainly. But he can't find the connecting threads to the rest of his life. For all its worth, YES has never enticed Manny to bring in enough of his Brooklyn life that he's been able to bridge the two. The program makes real efforts to be a place that welcomes everybody: it offers teens who are in far more dire straits than Manny perks like free food and emergency services like housing assistance and addiction-treatment referrals, and these incentives bring a diverse crowd through the drop-in center's doors, many of them straight from the pier. But Manny feels lost in the shuffle, in neither enough crisis nor enough comfort to benefit from what the program has to offer. As a result, YES and Andy and Melissa and his new queer life all remain miles away from life back on Eastern Parkway. Wherever he turns, he still chafes against that dreadful schism: the blackness of his Brooklyn life, the whiteness of his gay Manhattan one.

Even when he and Jason go out, the parties they can usually get into are filled with white kids from Long Island. That's certainly the story at Kurfew, which is always packed with blond teenyboppers and the people who adore them. Another of their regular spots is the Hole, a deliberately sleazy joint with lax enough rules that the boys' fake IDs get them in. Again, it's a fun scene but one where Manny and Jason and their crew stand out as black dots in a sea of white. Tonight, standing here on the piers and tossing off relaxed greetings to the friends Jason is sharing with him, Manny feels entirely different. The great black/gay divide of his life falls easily away. And if he feels at all out of place, it's not owing to either his race or his sexuality but rather to his reserved, new-kid-on-the-block demeanor.

That naïveté relative to Jason had, however, presented its own steady and growing discomfort all year.

Their relationship had taken a sudden turn right as Manny started ninth grade. They'd spent the summer apart, Manny in Puerto Rico and Jason home in Brooklyn, and by the time they

came back together puberty had worked a good bit of its mysterious magic on both of their bodies. "There was a significant development, physically, for both of us," Manny remembers. "We
were young men, on a whole different level." It wasn't all physical, though. Suddenly they also shared a matured understanding of what it was they were doing together, of the idea that they
had a relationship that was distinct from their other friendships.
They went to the movies together and didn't let others tag along.
They kept each other informed of their whereabouts. They presumed upon one another's time.

And they started to have anal sex. Today, Manny doesn't even
remember much about the first time it happened—long before
they found their way to Prospect Park and sex work; the only detail he's retained is that it seemed a natural, easy progression.
He more recalls how throughout this period Jason—now heading toward his late teens and long since dropped out of school
—seemed a different person, unsettlingly altered in ways both
identifiable and not. If the sex felt natural, Jason's posture
within it didn't. He suddenly knew how to do things with their
bodies, possessed a technical facility that outpaced Manny's
blind groping. He even talked about it differently, with specific
and explicit language for the things they did. For Jason, the exploratory stage that had begun with Manny's unsubtle come-
ons during sleepovers a couple of years prior was done.

"He had this whole other vocabulary, it was just a whole
brand-new thing, which I guess I found kind of hot," Manny explains. "But I also knew that something changed." He pauses
and twists his face through an ongoing effort to label Jason's
still-ephemeral shift. Failing, he shakes it off and moves on. "I
guess that was fine for me because I was like, 'Great, this is how
it happens. This is what's up.'" *It* being the journey to sexual
adulthood, to a more firm terrain for the behavioral side of his
homosexuality than he'd yet found.

Meanwhile, Manny's mom had lost her job right around the

time of his and Jason's reengagement. Cassandra took the set-back hard, and she slid into what would be a lasting, recurring depression. Manny reacted by hiding out in Jason's apartment every evening to avoid Cassandra's downward pull. As it was, their relationship had been on a steady decline since way back when she took him to the shrink out at St. John's University. Ever since, Cassandra had kept Manny at a careful distance that he was increasingly uninterested in closing. She seemed to be going through the motions of motherhood, trying to shape him into the image of a young black Puerto Rican man, but never able to really commit to the tumult of maternity.

It's like the way she handled the whole gay thing.

Enamored with the new queer identity he'd been cobbling together with Andy at the gay community center, Manny de-cided it was time to come out to Cassandra. He'd never been particularly concerned about keeping it from her, but at the same time he never felt he had anything concrete to offer by way of proof—someone he could point to as the person he loved and who loved him back. And the lines had always been so blurry with Jason, so he'd waited. Plus, Cassandra had always been skittish about Manny's sexuality. She put him in Boy Scouts. She had him take boxing lessons. She made him play baseball, which he was actually pretty good at, until he quit to join the chorus. "She was doing all these things to boost up my mas-culinity," Manny complains. But in ninth grade, with his new identity and things gelling with Jason, enough was enough. "I felt like I had to sort of put my foot down."

And the whole thing in fact went down about as gracefully as a foot stomp. He'd been out running around with either Ja-son or Andy, and when he walked into the apartment he found Cassandra splayed out on the couch. Maybe it was the abrupt transition between his worlds, from the increasingly comfort-able streets back into the shaky, confusing realm of home. Or maybe it was just something in the way she looked at him.

Whatever prompted it, Manny knew this was the moment. He took a few steps through the door, dropped his backpack next to the couch, and blurted out, "Mom, I'm gay."

There was a pregnant pause as the two stared each other down. Then Cassandra put on her social work hat and tentatively pushed forward. "Are you sure?" she asked.

"Yeah, I'm sure," Manny shot back. "I don't want to talk about it. I just need you to deal with it. It is what it is."

And with that, he walked on by her and went into his room. The conversation was closed, and would remain so for years. She'd bait him with the occasional sidelong remark, something flirting with homophobia, and he'd rise up in return; there'd be a fight. But beyond these flashes, Manny never pursued it further and Cassandra was all too happy to let it lie. She kept her comfortable distance from this emotional quagmire of her son's, just as she did with all his others.

Or that's how Manny understood it, anyway. He'd always felt she avoided his internal life and he took this as just another example. So when she lost her job and sunk into a depression, he returned the favor by withdrawing to Jason's apartment downstairs, where the two could push their own bond forward free of parental meddling.

And that's also where he and Jason started drinking and generally toying around with insobriety. They'd cue up choice selections from Jason's massive musical canon, play video games, and get silly drunk. It was plain fun, and like all things in Manny's life, he soon developed big ambitions around it. He tried on intoxicants like he was shopping for just the right outfit to match his precocious-outsider posture. He had long ago tested out pot, but for reasons he still can't fully articulate he'd hated the high. Something about feeling like his body and his mind had taken on lives of their own, about losing a firm, controlling grip on his surroundings. That hardly appealed to Manny. And while the drinking wasn't bad, there wasn't much cachet in it, nothing exceptional or adventurous, nothing to elevate him beyond the teenage hoi polloi.

Ecstasy, however, held promise. Watching and reading pop ular media, he'd come to understand ecstasy as the eighth sign of the apocalypse. Warnings about the drug had been widely and breathlessly broadcast: Here was the latest thing the bad kids were doing behind their parents' backs. So when one of the Long Island clubbers offered Manny a hit of ecstasy at Kurfew, he eagerly accepted.

The experience was a nightmare. It was like taking everything bad about pot and ratcheting it up to extremes. Also known by its technical name MDMA, ecstasy is a mood elevator. It mucks around with brain chemicals to release serotonin and create a euphoric feel that intensifies a range of sensations and emotions. Most dealers cut it with speed as well, and the combination makes the drug ideal for clubs with lots of flashing lights, pulsating music, and bodies bumping and grinding against one another for hours on end. You can completely lose yourself in the moment, allow the sensations to overwhelm you and drive you to drop your guard and let go. These were not things Manny was looking for. "I had no idea what I was doing," he complains. "I didn't know where I was or what I was touching." And the next day he was a wreck.

Still, as awful as the ecstasy experience had been in real time, the aftermath was pretty close to euphoric. Manny and Jason's outings were always a source of excitement, producing all manner of drama that the boys could lie around and needle over in the days and weeks between each adventure. Did you see what so and so did when he got there? What about when I danced with that one guy? And where'd you go during that second DJ set? Dropping ecstasy was ideal grist for this mill, and Manny actually rushed to school the next morning to tell Lisa all about it. He walked into gym class and created a stir with his pasty, ghostly skin, dehydrated and spent from the seven- or eight-hour ecstasy trip. He pulled Lisa aside and delivered a full-bore gush of an explanation.

"Oh my God, *Jason!* I love him. We had a *crazy* night, but I love him!"

It wasn't the first or last time he'd pour it on like that for Lisa. She'd indulge him for a while, then launch into her own drama about her dad's girlfriend and how much she hated the lady. This was their routine. She was the only person at school he let into his Brooklyn world. She'd never actually meet Jason, or physically trespass on that part of Manny's life. But he nevertheless tested out an emotional bridge between the two with her. And she liked Manny and his exotic adventures, so she'd indulge the stories, to a point. At least till it was her turn to unload.

So they all spent weeks dissecting the ecstasy mishap. Manny and Lisa at school; Jason and Manny at home. Manny would go on and on about how he didn't like losing control like that, how he needed something to party with that let him keep his wits about him. He would never really suss out just how far ahead of him Jason was by this point. When had Jason started tricking? Where had he picked up the extra drug experience? How long had he been acting naive, and why did he suddenly decide to stop? Whatever the answers, Manny never got them. But about a month into the ecstasy conversation, Jason revealed that he knew just what Manny was looking for, at least when it came to drugs.

"Why don't you just try cocaine?" Jason asked him one night as they were slouching around his apartment.

Manny flinched. "Well, I don't know." He didn't get it. Coke was something adults did, something he'd heard about going on in the sorts of crowds his adoptive dad, Christian, ran around with in the Manhattan art scene.

Jason pushed on past the doubtful looks. "I think that's what you want, based on what you're saying."

"I don't want to be doing no old-man shit."

"No, it's OK. I tried it the other day."

Huh? What the hell? Manny reeled as he took in this remark and all its implied betrayals. Here was proof that he wasn't crazy, that there were indecipherable changes in Jason, things going on outside of his reach. "Wait a minute. When did you try this shit? Why didn't you tell me?"

The answers didn't actually matter. Manny was already sold. The only question that he really needed answered looked to the future rather than the past: where could he get some?

But that was the rub. However long Jason had been doing coke, he wasn't yet savvy enough to track it down on demand. It took some doing, asking around and making their intentions known and, well, gathering up money, because the stuff wouldn't be cheap. And it wasn't like ecstasy or pot, you couldn't count on those Long Island kids to have something like this. They'd just have to lie in wait and, if they were lucky, they'd stumble across it at a party someplace. Someplace like the Christopher Street pier.

The dance showdown hasn't officially started yet, but freelance dance-offs are unfolding all around, and the swelling crowd on the pier has swallowed up Jason. Manny stands alone, watching the kids contort their bodies into the dramatic, rapid flying motions of voguing. Unlike most of his peers, he's not at all interested in joining one of the informal gay social clubs—called "houses"—that voguing grew up out of and that organize events like this one, and he certainly can't see himself out there voguing. But he loves the performance of it nonetheless. It looks as much like a choreographed martial arts fight as it does dancing. The performers' arms and legs pop as their joints lock into sharp right angles, all while squatting into duck walks that in turn morph into gravity-defying high kicks. It all culminates in a sudden, midpose freeze-frame, often involving a bone-shattering backward drop onto whatever unforgiving ground is beneath. And yet those who vogue well maintain a sensual grace within all of this. Their chopping and stomping and dropping somehow feels curvaceous.

Jason returns and sidles up alongside Manny. Smiling, he dangles before Manny's face the catch that he'd gone off to claim: a small cellophane baggie of coke. It's a relatively tiny serving in reality, just enough for each of them to snort a line or two and stay jazzed for maybe forty-five minutes at best.

"Oh shit!" Manny exclaims. Finally, this is it. After all the talk and the anxiety and the buildup, he'll finally get to try this stuff out for himself. Of course, it quickly strikes him that he doesn't really know *how* to try it. He nevertheless confidently takes the little baggie from Jason, pinches open its ziplock seal, and moves to toss it back into his mouth like it's Pixy Stix candy. Jason mercifully intervenes.

There's a right way to do this, he explains, and walks Manny over to one of the big concrete slabs lying around near the nascent construction site. He finds a relatively splinter-free board and rests it on top of the concrete, then pours the coke out of its baggie and onto their makeshift tray. He takes out the pocketknife he's always got on him and starts fussing around with the powder, arranging it into two mounds and then two thin lines. Manny's impatient with the process, and thinks to himself that this is an awful lot of work just to get a buzz. But when Jason passes him the dollar bill he's rolled up into a tight straw, Manny copies his boy's moves and snorts his line deep into his nostril.

"It was just like"—Manny bugs out his eyes and slacks his jaw to re-create the wonder he felt at the time—"it was a sensation that I never had before." And Jason hadn't lied about how it'd feel. He achieved the euphoria of getting all fucked up but still maintained awareness and control—indeed, he felt even more control than when sober, as if he could do anything, conquer any task. And whatever self-consciousness he had about

dancing and getting into the party vibe out there was long gone.
To the contrary, he wanted to dance to everything. "I was
hooked," he gushes, referring not to some simple physical addiction but, rather, to a far deeper emotional pull. "Instantly
hooked."

Later that night, sobriety comes crashing in when Jason explains that getting anything more than the tiny serving they'd
snorted would cost sixty bucks. They both realize there's no way
they can afford something like that on a regular basis. Jason's
parents have good enough jobs that they can slide him some
cash, but not enough to support them both at prices that high.
And Manny's mom is out of work and broke. He sometimes can
get money from Christian, but these days he and Christian don't
see much of each other. So that's just that, he figures, the coke
thing will have to be catch-as-catch-can.

They go back to square one. Once again, they put the word
out that they're interested, keep their eyes peeled at parties, and
try to worm their way into the circles where folks do things like
coke. And in this way they score more often than they expect,
and like anything else the more they search the better they get
at finding. It's all just a great deal of fun, frankly, not just the
score but the hunt, too. The whole process is terribly social, driving them to meet new people and check out new scenes. And
when they get hold of the prize, they take it at parties like the
voguing showdown on the pier, places packed with other young
people, full of warmth and revelry. Within a couple of months
they're doing coke at least a couple times a week—certainly
whenever they go out but, increasingly, when they're sitting
around alone in Jason's apartment as well. Ultimately, it both
prompts and enables their excursions into sex work.

The most thorough research available on risk and youth is
probably the U.S. Centers for Disease Control and Prevention's
biannual survey of teens, with the literal-minded title Youth

Risk Behavior Survey, or YRBS. It's a treasure trove for all manner of researchers, as it asks thousands of anonymous high
school students dozens of questions about themselves and the
potentially unhealthy things they do. It asks about how much
exercise the kids get and what kinds of diet they have. It asks if
they smoke or use other forms of tobacco. It asks about sex—
how often they have it, at what age, under what circumstances,
and with what sort of safety precautions. And it asks about
drugs and alcohol, again drilling down on the details of when,
where, and how. So you can learn, for instance, that four out of
five students who rode bikes in 2005 never wore helmets, and
that black males were particularly unlikely to wear one. Or that
Hispanic males were the most likely to have tried cocaine, with
a whopping 15 percent saying they'd done so.

But the YRBS has its limits. For one, you've got to be both
enrolled in and actually showing up for school to have your answers counted. And for all its probing around sex, gender, and
race, what the survey doesn't ask is if you consider yourself
gay, lesbian, bisexual, transgender, or even just unsure on the
matter. Which means, on the question of risk, researchers interested in gay youth have been left groping around in the dark,
cobbling together small, localized data sets in an effort to understand. One place they've turned for help is the state of Massachusetts. Each state acts under CDC guidance to conduct its
own YRBS, which the feds then patch together to form a national picture. And in 1995, Massachusetts added questions
about sexual orientation to its survey. Given the results, it's hard
to imagine how other states genuinely interested in youth risk
behavior haven't followed suit.

In 2003, 6 percent of Massachusetts' students identified
themselves either as being gay or having had some same-sex
sexual contact in their lives. You've got to look hard at the rest of
the survey to find something public health officials consider
risky that those gay students aren't doing more of than their
peers, and by wide margins.

The survey makes it clear, for instance, that Jason and Manny's quest for insobriety was hardly unique. Gay kids were more likely to use every form of intoxicant, and to do so with greater intensity. Half of them said they smoked, which was double the general student population. Sixty percent said they drank, and 44 percent did so in "binges," compared to 26 percent overall. Half also said they currently used illegal drugs —ecstasy, pot, coke—compared to 29 percent of the overall population.

The survey also found gay kids' lives to be riddled with violence. A quarter of them said they carried a weapon (compared to 13 percent of students overall) and more than four in ten said they had been in at least one fight in the previous year (compared to three in ten overall). Counter to what most would expect, they were also far more likely to have been in a gang than straight kids, by a margin of 23 percent to 9 percent. Other answers suggest they carry weapons and join gangs because they feel they need protection: 22 percent said they'd been threatened with or injured by a weapon at school (compared to just 5 percent overall) and 42 percent said they'd been bullied, twice that of the general student population.

Gay teens also had far more active sex lives than their peers. More than three-quarters said they'd had sex, and one in five said they'd done it by the time they were thirteen years old. Comparatively, 39 percent of the overall population said they'd had sex and just 4 percent had done so as preteens. Gay kids were also more than three times as likely to say they'd had at least four sexual partners as the overall population and, in another counterintuitive fact, were twice as likely to have either been pregnant or have gotten someone pregnant. But here again, violence is pervasive. Forty-one percent said they'd been forced into sexual contact against their will, compared to 8 percent overall. Thirty percent said they'd experienced some sort of dating violence, compared to 9 percent overall.

The litany of increased risk goes on and on in this fashion.

Gay kids are less likely to participate in sports, more likely to be obese, more likely to skip school. They're even less likely to wear seatbelts.

And none of this has escaped the nation's culture wars surrounding sexuality, either. Religious Right organizations that argue homosexuality is a disorder—one that can and should be treated and cured—say all this risk is just one more sign of the condition's depravity. In July 1998, after a landmark study mined the initial Massachusetts YRBS data to tease out the gay-specific trends, conservatives pounced. In a full-page *New York Times* ad, a coalition of "ex-gay" movement groups urged the nation to rally behind "hope and healing for homosexuals." Among other things, the ad cited the Massachusetts data as reasons for the need to treat homosexuality, declaring the survey revealed "a high degree of destructive behavior among homosexuals, including alcohol, drug abuse, and emotional or physical violence." It went on to interpret these evils, arguing that they represent "the visible response to a broken heart." The ad ran in major dailies around the country throughout the month.

Chicago's Dr. Robert Garofalo was the study's lead researcher. He had been working with gay youth since 1995, both as a clinician and as a researcher, and he countered then and maintains now that all of this risk actually stems from the sort of "isolation and rejection" described in GLSEN's surveys of gay high school students. To Garofalo, the YRBS is a terribly blunt tool for understanding risk, because it fails to examine the larger context in which these disembodied choices about sex and drugs are made. "I don't think 'risk' itself, in the way we talk about it, is particularly helpful. We talk about it in terms of pathology," Garofalo argues. But risk-taking is neither unusual nor inappropriate for adolescents. "Find me an adolescent that isn't an 'at-risk' adolescent and I'll show you one who isn't healthy," he quips. "All adolescents take risks. It's just about making those risks calculated."

And that's the rub for Garofalo—that gay kids are both more likely to get backed into a set of dangerous choices and, perhaps most importantly, are less likely to have someone with whom they identify available to help make those decisions in a calculated rather than haphazard manner. "It's the milieu, the environment that these kids live in," he says of young people like Jason and Manny. "The one thing that I think would help is to have some sort of adult role model to turn to." And yet his research shows that to be a woefully unlikely resource. He led a team that surveyed five hundred Chicago youth about a range of things, including whether they have "someone they look up to." The study was still unpublished in early 2007, but the preliminary findings were that a disproportionate share of the lesbian, gay, bisexual, and transgender kids said they did not. And among those who said they did in fact have someone, "by and large they were unavailable people—Beyoncé, Oprah, people who were not available to them" in any interpersonal way. That reality leaves young gay people wrestling with all of the commonplace but nonetheless difficult choices of adolescence on their own, with no standard to measure their personal calculations against. What's a gamble and what's a sure bet? What's a reasonable ante just to play? Are the stakes of letting this crush or this sexual encounter or this argument go by as great as they seem? Are they worth betting my health or my education or even my life for? Neither Jason nor Manny had any formula for deciphering answers to these questions. So they tended to just go all in.

"Come sit down, Manny."

Cassandra has just hung up the phone and, despite her calm, cool demeanor, it's clear to Manny there's a huge problem. She's in that placid state she always affects when the chaos of their life starts interrupting the normally distracting daily grind. And she's wearing the social worker face she uses when doing some unpleasant business. Manny braces himself.

"Your father had a heart attack this morning," Cassandra carefully explains. "He's no longer with us."

Manny hears the words, but he can't quite process their meaning. Christian is by now more of an idea than a real person. After Cassandra and Manny moved to Brooklyn, Christian had honored Cassandra's wishes and slowly withdrawn, and he eventually returned to London altogether. Manny still had sporadic contact with his adoptive dad, but Christian's role in his life had been more symbolic than practical for a good while, a theoretical placeholder for both emotional and financial support. Manny always leaned precariously on this imaginary crutch, and as Cassandra delivers her speech about death and loss, he feels his grip on the comforting fantasy slipping.

So he cuts her off. He'll get to the bottom of this himself, he figures. He snatches up the phone and starts frantically dialing. He starts with Christian himself, calling their former London home over and over again, getting no answer. He moves on to Christian's brother—still no answer. Undeterred, he keeps calling all day, rotating between the different homes of Christian's family in London and listening as the other line rings endlessly.

Finally, Christian's father picks up; they don't have a pleasant conversation.

Manny's not crazy, he's known all day not to expect a warm embrace, and it's not like he has any desire to rejoin Christian's family. He just wants someone to acknowledge he once belonged there, at least in Christian's mind, and that they've got to include him in whatever will come next. His former grandfather, however, has answered the phone with the sole purpose of disabusing Manny of this idea.

"You are not welcome in this family anymore," he says before abruptly hanging up.

The next few weeks are tough. The funny thing is that Christian's actual death doesn't shake Manny up so much; he hasn't even cried about it. But thinking about the conversation with his onetime grandfather, a man he's despised most of his life, brings body-convulsing tears of grief. Manny focuses all of this confusing emotional energy onto his stuff—his old pictures, kiddie pillows, toys, and the random detritus of a childhood he'd left behind in London years ago. They're things that had never been important enough for him to claim, or maybe keeping them in London had made him feel like he had a beachhead in that world. He's not even sure they still exist, frankly. Nonetheless, he grows increasingly desperate to get them back now. They are concrete, tangible representations of a past that makes less and less sense to him every day. They are his history, and he wants to possess them. But he never will. He'll never even have another direct conversation with his grandfather.

"It was so absurd," Manny says in summing up the time. "That whole time period was just absurd." After all, for the first nine years of his life, he was told that Christian was his father.

That was, of course, a half-truth that Manny himself had gradually rebelled against in the years since he and Cassandra moved to Brooklyn. Even before he began constructing his queer identity, he'd gradually cobbled together a racial one that fit with the new world he'd been thrust into. From the first, he'd felt weird not just around the Haitian and black kids at his elementary school but also interacting with the black and brown kids in his building. Reflecting on those awkward years, he talks as if he constructed his racial identity as consciously as he did his sexual one. He seemed to get that there was a certain aesthetic to being black—whether African American or Caribbean, which is a terribly fine distinction in Brooklyn—and to understand that it was a style and form he had not mastered. He got blackness as a concept, and his voracious reading helped him obtain a deep understanding of race and how it shapes the world. But the bizarre circumstances of his earliest years left him confused as to how exactly all that played out in his own life. It's almost as if he had to teach himself to be black—and that lesson meant, in no small part, distancing himself from Christian.

But throughout, Manny had nonetheless kept close the stabilizing ideas Christian represented. He'd been a potential secret escape, not just from the sober economic realities of life with his mother but from the racial ones as well. Now, with Christian dead and his family definitively cutting whatever links may have been conceivable, a grim new reality came crashing in for Manny. The potential for sudden change was gone—no more wistful London past, no more fanciful future of financial support, no more alternate lives. And no more false superiority over all those people—black and white—who looked at him askance and jumped to conclusions about who and what he is. Christian's death dashed all of these notions and jarred Manny into stark clarity about his life. He couldn't get past the obvious —"You're just a black kid on the street."

A whole lot follows from that conclusion. For one, all that jazz his teachers talk about his potential—or that he tells himself about his potential—doesn't amount to much. Sure, he can make it someplace, but not how they're thinking. The rules weren't written for him and all his blackness and gayness and rootlessness. "That's why I had to prepare myself to be on my own. Because the vision that all these teachers and people had for me was just—" He stops, frustrated still, and fumbles for the words. "It was not the life that I was leading."

Among other things, the life that he was leading involved a growing coke habit.

Manny and Jason have been cultivating their new pastime all spring, as Manny has grown less and less interested in whatever it was that had caught his attention back at the beginning of ninth grade and thus has spent less and less time at school. By now they're getting tweaked a couple times a week. With all the chaos around Christian's death, Manny's more interested in boosting that up than ratcheting it down, but this takes money —money that Jason has been largely responsible for providing thus far. Given that neither of the boys is gainfully employed, however, the question of resources is an increasingly pressing one. It's the coke, yes, but it's the lifestyle too—running around the city with his YES friends, clubbing with Jason, filling days overflowing with time that other kids spend in school. Freedom like this costs.

Manny knows that, but he hasn't given it much real thought —that's part of the Christian fantasy, that things big and small will always work themselves out somehow. Jason, always more grounded, has on the other hand been preoccupied with the matter for a while now. This is his personality. He doesn't fret and fuss over things the way Manny does; he identifies a problem and sets about solving it. And so, not too many weeks after Christian's death, late one night as the boys are lounging on his apartment floor doing the usual, Jason decides to let Manny in on his new Prospect Park hustle.

"Yo, let's go to the park."

SEVEN

"Show me your dick."

No problem, Manny thinks. It's just the kind of request he's happy getting from his tricks, and Jason's been making sure he stays in this easy, show-me realm of prostitution since they started working together in the park. That's Jason's MO here; he's the caretaker not just for Manny but for all the regulars that come through to hang out and work. He brings in condoms for everybody, makes sure Manny carries his pocketknife, helps Manny build a client base of regulars who aren't too whacked out. As for Manny, he's figured out by now that this is where Jason learned all that sexy new stuff they've been doing when they mess around—and he's picking up some new ideas himself, like this business of fetishes. He'd never thought that people could get turned on by the sort of quirky requests guys make of him here. Feet? Who's turned on by feet? Or by just looking at his dick? That's not sex, Manny thinks, and it's this conceit that makes the whole exchange palatable. Yes, these guys are paying him for the use of his body, but not in any way that he thinks about in relationship to actual desire. So while the johns might be having sex of some sort, *he's* not, because all he's doing is showing this dude his penis.

Such distinctions are important to Manny, not just because they give some order to what he's doing, but because they help him make sense of Jason's behavior. While hanging around the gay community center's youth program, Manny's learned all about STDs and HIV and all the physical dangers you can encounter with a sex life as wide open as he and Jason are getting into. But that's not such a big concern, because there are clear-cut ways to prevent disease—don't swallow when you're giving head; do your best to inspect the guy for warts or sores; and keep a regular eye out for problem signs on yourself too, like pubic lice or puss or other assorted grossness. Of far greater concern to Manny is that Jason not share his cum with anybody else. That's the dividing line, and it's as good a place as any to draw a contrasting boundary between what he and Jason have been doing together in their parents' apartments and what they're now doing separately here in the park. "His semen was so important to me," Manny explains. "It was the thing that made me special." So the boys agree on a hard-and-fast rule: gotta use condoms in the park, always, no exceptions. The fact that this dictum also limits their STD risk to nonlethal infections is a mere lucky coincidence. And the fact that Manny's own safety within the relationship is dependent upon Jason's honoring that agreement doesn't cross his mind—obviously, he can trust the guy he loves.

Manny even insists on using rubbers when he sucks dick. Some of the guys grumble about it, some even stiff him a little on the money as a result. But for the most part it's not the actual blow job his tricks want, anyway—it's not like he's very good at it, after all—it's the idea they're paying for, the erotic notions embodied in his youth or his blackness or both, knelt down and wrapped around their penis. Most of those guys could care less if he puts a rubber over it first.

These tidy rules carry Manny and Jason through most of the spring and into the summer before Manny's tenth-grade year, tumbling along in their comfortable routine. A couple of months into it, Manny finally has to start getting fucked in order to make any real money, but by then he's ready for it, or so he thinks. He and Jason have done it enough that he knows how to take it, and looking back later he won't even be able to remember the first time he had to do it in the park. It is something of a nonevent in the grander scheme of things. It does start to put a cramp in the boys' private sex life, though—"We were just so spent," Manny laments—and submitting to the act makes him more physically vulnerable, of course. But he even figures out how to deal with that pretty quickly: whenever the moment comes, he discreetly pulls from his pocket the flip-blade knife Jason gave him to fend off robberies. As he yanks his pants down to his knees and turns his back to the john, he cups the knife in his palm and wraps his hand around his dick, acting like he's jacking off. It's a simple enough maneuver that no one ever notices, and it successfully puts him at ease.

The real trouble Manny faces in the park isn't the sex; it's that, even with the coke fueling him socially, he still feels like a freak alongside all of Jason's friends, most of whom are there for way more than the sex work. The hours they spend in the park are often the best part of an otherwise trying day. Some are homeless and sleeping in shelters or on the street, most are surfing from one temporary housing situation to the next—staying with an auntie, a cousin, a boyfriend's cousin; anything to get out of an abusive home. They come here to unwind and relax, to let their guard down. So in between meeting johns, they sit around playing cards and talking shit about whatever drama's going on in the scene on the Christopher Street pier and in the Village. They practice voguing. They meet boyfriends. But Manny's just too scared for all that playtime. He keeps to himself.

And it isn't just the sex work that has him on pins and needles; it's all these people, too. On one hand, it's a relief to be there, just like it is to be out on the pier, because he does feel a greater kinship than when he's in whiter queer spaces. But at the same time he's still an oddball. He can be cordial, but in the end he has nothing in common with the other kids here and sees them, frankly, as downright bizarre, with their strange lingo and their contortionist dances and all their utterly un-apologetic queerness. Where the hell do they all come from, anyway? He never sees these guys around Brooklyn outside the park. And what do any of their stories and anecdotes have to do with him? Surely, he'd think while standing around listening to them carry on, nobody here has read the newspaper today.

So he keeps his distance, and he tries not to reveal his dis-comfort by holding himself out as the quiet, introspective one. Everybody else reads that as him being butch and authentically manly; they find it attractive, and they embrace him even if he can't embrace them.

But on the whole, the Prospect Park plan seems to Manny to be working out—though he suspects Cassandra's gotten the idea in her head that he's dealing drugs, or at least involved with drug dealers. After all, how else could she explain how a fifteen-year-old ends up with as much pocket money as Manny always has? She could certainly never conjure up the idea that he might be a prostitute. But whatever. Cassandra has her own prob-lems—not least of which is dealing with dramatic mood swings that would later be diagnosed as depression—and Manny is happy to exploit them in order to keep her out of his business. He's got this situation under control.

From the moment nineteen-year-old Julius stepped off the Greyhound bus from north Florida into the hustle and bustle of Times Square, he felt his grip on the sort of control Manny figured he'd captured slipping away. His goal had been to break out of the emotional and physical bondage he'd been mired in down South, and that much he'd accomplished. He was now free, to be sure, and right up until his abrupt departure from the city three years later, he'd profess himself to be living out the best years of his life. But his was an odd sort of liberation. The alternately abusive and confusing life of north Florida no longer held him hostage, but making it on his own with few resources or life skills would mean learning lots of lessons the hard way.

Midtown Manhattan is an insane cacophony of exhausting stimulus that takes a lot of adjusting to. Never mind fighting your way through the throngs of people cramming the sidewalk all hours of the day and night; forget the intimidating hassle of figuring out how to use the crowded, pushy subways; just digesting all of the blaring, flashing media you're bombarded by is enough to make you need a midday nap. It was a lot for the newly liberated Julius, too, and he stayed at the comfy Gershwin Hotel much longer than he had meant to. He kept a long-term rental for a few weeks before finally migrating to a much more affordable international students' hostel, where he stayed for a couple weeks more. But barely more than a month after his arrival in the city, Julius was entirely broke. He checked into Covenant House, and for the remainder of his stay in New York his independence tied him to shelters and other temporary housing arrangements.

"My first couple of weeks at Covenant House were really traumatic," he testified in a statement to federal investigators, part of a probe into his foster family's scams. In recounting his post-Florida exploits in those legal documents, Julius stated that he was subject at Covenant House to just the sort of abuse gay-youth-services providers charge is commonplace in the Catholic shelter. "I was robbed and all my clothes were stolen. All the other kids made fun of me. I got in a fight with one guy who beat me up pretty badly. I had never been so lonely in my life."

For Julius, however, that torture was but a temporary part of his time in the shelter, and he considered it a small price to pay for the family he slowly developed at Covenant House and in the streets of New York City. "I made a lot of friends at Covenant House," he testified, "who are still my friends today. My three

months there were beautiful and I wouldn't trade them for anything in the world." This duality would be typical of Julius's New
York life—trauma in one moment, freedom and belonging in
the next, or often happening concurrently and in the same
space. Covenant House is, for instance, also where he learned
how to do the sex work he'd regularly turn to in order to finance
his freedom.

Still, the plainly harsh realities of his New York life do nothing to alter the equally clear fact that Julius's time here was the
most authentic he'd ever spent. From the moment he walked
out of the Port Authority, he burst into a new, truer self. It may
not have been the life he had imagined as he climbed onto the
Greyhound in north Florida, but it was in fact his own, one he'd
built from scratch and one in which he made his own decisions.
Even if surviving in New York still meant making tough choices,
like those about when and how to sell his body, he nonetheless
made them of his own volition. And like thousands of black
and Latino gay, lesbian, bisexual, and transgender people, Julius
both discovered and cultivated his new self inside a unique,
decades-old subculture organized around surrogate families
known as "houses." The "flamboyant" youth he longingly spied
playing around in front of Covenant House as he pulled into
Times Square were part of this scene, and once he got his footing at the shelter, Julius quickly immersed himself in it.

The history of the "house ball" scene is still being written, but
most observers agree it has its roots in the drag balls of the
Harlem Renaissance. Throughout the early twentieth century,
black Harlem played a curious role for the rest of New York City:
it was a place where white folks secreted themselves after dark
to break the rules of civility they felt bound by in their day-
time lives. Sexual fluidity and experimentation in general were
among the many taboos whites came uptown to flaunt, and the
era's more daring homosexual white men cavorted at a host of

gay-welcoming nightclubs with the black artists and intellectuals who were similarly engaged in a mini sexual revolution, the details of which remain clouded to history. Academics and rumormongers alike continue to speculate about and debate over the sexuality of some of the Harlem Renaissance's biggest names: Langston Hughes and Countee Cullen and Zora Neale Hurston and others. At least one Renaissance artist, the poet and painter Richard Bruce Nugent, was brazen enough in 1926 to write openly about same-sex love and desire, and his similarly open colleague Wallace Thurman penned an infamous 1932 send-up of the Renaissance's social scene that depicted an easy acceptance of homosexuality. Both the black and white participants in this sexual milieu came together for raucous gatherings that began as costume parties and transformed into events at which partygoers dressed in drag and competed in fashion shows of sorts; the most famous of these parties, held at the Rockland Palace in Upper West Harlem, became known as "the faggots ball," according to gay-Harlem historian Michael Henry Adams.

But as with many things in the Harlem Renaissance, the white men who held the drag-ball scene's purse strings maintained their privilege of power even as they sought refuge from its constraints in their downtown life. Frank León Roberts, a young black and gay writer who both studies and participates in today's house-ball scene, says black participants chafed under the power imbalance and, by the 1960s, had carved out exclusively black versions of the balls. "However, the cultural and political landscape of Harlem—specifically the neighborhood's earlier carefree 'acceptance' of drag culture—had changed drastically," Roberts writes in an online history. "The balls became a more dangerous pastime pleasure. The balls began to be held as early as 3, 4, or 5 a.m.—a tradition that continues to this day—in order to make it safer for participants to travel the streets of Harlem with high-heels and feathers."

In the late 1970s and throughout the 1980s, these black-specific balls gave birth to the "houses" that still organize the scene today. The houses, each of which is usually named after a high-end fashion designer—there's the House of Blahnik, the House of Revlon, the House of Milan, and so on—are organized around a shared belonging rather than any physical space. Ball veterans reign as house "mothers"—often but not necessarily transgender women or drag queens—and as house "fathers"—sometimes transgender men or hyperbutch lesbians, but often gay men who style themselves in classic black or Latin masculinity. Young men, women, and transgender folks seek out a given house to join, often based on a friend's membership, and then become "children" of the house mother and father's family, which can encompass anything from a small, tight-knit circle of a dozen people to hundreds of members spanning several cities. The houses take turns hosting massive dance and fashion competitions, modern-day versions of the Harlem Renaissance balls. These vibrant all-night parties feature hours and hours of successive competitions in which members of each house walk a makeshift runway and square off in categories meant to demonstrate skill for passing as one caricature or another—"realness" as a Wall Street executive, a supermodel, an oil-rig worker—or ability to show off various styles, from being a "sex siren" to having a clean-cut, pretty-girl look to just having an unclockable presentation of a gender other than the one you were assigned at birth. These show-me categories are interspersed with heated dance-offs like the one Manny and Jason watched on the Christopher Street pier, in which the houses' youngest members try to outvogue one another, jumping and spinning in their homegrown dance style over a rapid beat and the scat-like rap of the event's MC.

To Roberts, the house-ball scene blossomed in the 1970s and 1980s as a gay answer to the same political and economic forces that gave birth to hip-hop culture in New York City. Seeking an outlet for the frustrations and pressures of living in increasingly rotted out urban areas like East New York, straight guys and girls released their frustrations in the music and dance of the street parties that grew into today's multibillion-dollar hip-hop industry. Gay youth, meanwhile, reclaimed and remade the gender and sexuality play of the Harlem Renaissance. "The 'houses' became underground social networks by and for urban black gay people," Roberts writes. "By 1980, three houses emerged straight out of Brooklyn: the House of Omni, the House of Ebony, and the House of Chanel. These houses were comprised of mostly men, many of whom preferred masculine aesthetics over drag. The creation of 'houses' transformed the drag circuit forever as newer populations, some of which would have never been attracted to drag balls, entered into the community. A rich taxonomy of gender personas and identities flooded in: thugged out hustlers who were 'new' to gay culture, butch lesbians with erotic attachments to gay men, bootleg black designers and fashionistas eager to put their garments 'to test' in a new, urban scene."

The scene is also one of few parts of the black and Latino gay experience that has drawn popular attention. The 1990 documentary film *Paris Is Burning* took viewers inside the late '80s version of New York City's balls, focusing in on a handful of members in now-legendary houses like Xtravaganza and Ninja. The film's real power is in its up-close look at the way in which the houses function as surrogate families for poor, often homeless youth whose shared bloodlines with their parents and siblings aren't enough to bind them. But many in today's ball scene look back at *Paris Is Burning* as a blemish, and they cringe at what they feel is an overly negative portrayal—strung-out drag queens, kids stealing and running scams, subculture celebrities confessing self-hating emotions like wanting to bleach their skin white. "That's a part of the community and it needs to be talked about," says Michael Roberson, who's been a "ball kid" since he was a young man coming out in early-1990s New Jersey, and who now works on black gay and AIDS community-organizing campaigns. "But there was never really a balance," he frets about the film. "Nobody in there talks about the houses working and contributing to the community."

The houses and balls have also changed in many ways since *Paris Is Burning* was filmed. What started as a largely New York phenomenon has taken up roots in just about every city with a large black population—Philly, D.C., Chicago, Detroit, Atlanta, and on and on, even spreading as far west as Los Angeles. Roberts estimates that as of early 2007 there were more than one hundred active houses in thirteen cities around the country. The growth has been dynamic: as black and Latino gay New Yorkers have migrated to other cities, they have started up first new chapters of existing houses and then new houses altogether. They hold balls and promote them nationwide, drawing visitors and establishing their new towns as hospitable places for black and Latino gays. Which in turn draws more migrants and more houses and more balls. And they've also grown alongside a circuit of black-specific gay pride festivals, many of which now have coinciding balls that draw thousands of revelers from around the country. "One of the most brilliant things about the ballroom scene is how they mobilize community," says Roberson, who has organized balls to coincide with New York City's own black gay pride festival. "Just a ball flyer, one ball flyer, can get people here from Chicago. It's the most amazing thing. People pass them around. Word of mouth at other balls. They call each other." And in recent years, they've turned to the Internet as well, establishing bulletin boards and Listservs to promote and review balls, but also simply to connect the increasingly disparate community. Of all the gay community's organizing efforts—black or white, male or female, political or social—the balls clearly stand among the most successful, sustained examples, all done in a largely organic manner with few resources by a group of primarily marginalized people.

Activists like Roberson have picked up on that remarkable fact and are trying to piggyback political and social change campaigns on the balls, working with the houses to interject HIV-prevention and education components. There have also been a number of thus far unsuccessful efforts to create an overarching, unifying structure—a kind of federation of houses—that would allow even more deliberate leveraging of the community's power. Gay Men's Health Crisis even created a house of its own, the House of Latex, with the explicit purpose of not just competing in balls but also using the informal network to promote healthy community.

Julius was an active Latex member during what he sees as his best New York months, spanning a year or so before he moved into the Crystal Street house in East New York. He was in what he describes as a healthy relationship—"a nine-month relationship, so I was sleeping with one person, largely monogamous; that was *nine months*"—and he had advanced from just receiving help at service groups targeting queer youth of color to also working at them as a peer educator and counselor, including as a mentor for younger Latex members and ball kids even outside of his house. "I love this scene," he'll gush. "I go and just vogue out to the music." It's a taxing style of dance, and he's sprained his ankle four times and dislocated his shoulder once. "The pain! Oh my god, just from voguing. I said, how do these bitches do it day in and day out?"

But he joined in and kept up just the same. More than that, really. In Latex and elsewhere, Julius stepped right into the center of whatever room he entered. Gone were the days of finding peace in the solitude of being banished to his foster family's garden shed, of quietly hiding out in the library during lunch hour or working alone in the yearbook office. In New York City, Julius was in the middle of things—the ringleader. "He was the life of the party," Justin remembers. Justin is a young, gay Mexican American who became one of Julius's closest friends while the two lived together in Harlem, during the pre–East

New York period that Julius most cherished. "He was one of the people who got me to come out of the shell that I had gone into."

Justin was nineteen at the time he met Julius, and he was struggling with both a growing coke habit and the depression that was fueling the abuse. He's a husky, round-faced guy with long black hair he keeps in a ponytail and all the physical signs of someone who spent his formative years in the raver scene. Piercings jut out all over his face—a fine, sparkly pin stuck through his left eyebrow; a ring looping through the side of his mustached lip; a bar cutting through his bearded chin, with two little white balls marking either end of the jewel. He speaks with a chill-dude, stoner cadence and seems like the type who would be hard to rile up; you know he's having a belly laugh not because he hoots and giggles in the way Julius would, but because his already broad smile stretches particularly wide across his face. That's the kind of smile he gets when he talks about his days with Julius in their four-person group-living apartment up on 149th Street. "It was a special time," he says, beaming. "We had our group, and it felt really good."

Justin was coming through a rocky period when he moved into the apartment, which was one of Green Chimneys' transitional-living setups, where gay youth between the ages of seventeen and twenty-one can stay together in small group homes and work with counselors to figure out how they can live self-sufficiently. Justin grew up with his parents and little sister in the East Village, and by the time he was fourteen years old he was spending all of his time in both the East and West Village street-kid scene. He'd begun by hanging out at the public sculpture known as "the Cube"—a ten-feet-tall steel block that stands askew on one of its points, at the bustling intersection of Astor Place and Lafayette Street, which has been the East Village's most iconic landmark since 1968. The tiny concrete square in

which the Cube sits has long been one of the primary hang-
outs for the city's disaffected, countercultural teens, from ravers
to goths to skateboarders. Fourteen-year-old Justin joined the
crowd there every day, mainly because he felt like a bizarre outsider on his family's Latino block a stone's throw away, and he
didn't know where else to go that he wouldn't be a weirdo because he was gay.

One day, a straight girl he was chilling out with said she was
heading down the street to the Hetrick-Martin Institute to get a
free meal. Justin hadn't heard of the place, but the institute had
been around since 1979, providing some of the most aggressive
—and controversial—social services in the country explicitly
aimed at gay kids like himself, including a small, city-funded
high school named the Harvey Milk School, after the pioneer-
ing San Francisco politician credited with being the first openly
gay man elected to public office. Hetrick-Martin sits just a few
doors down Astor Place from the Cube, and five days a week gay
kids from all over the city flock there to get a hot dinner and generally hang out in a safe space. The ragtag collection of hetero
outcasts from the Cube join in many days, too, so Justin followed along.

But he found way more than a meal at Hetrick-Martin. He
stumbled into a crowd of what he estimates to have been about
fifty queer teens like himself, and he was simply blown away to
learn that salvation had been sitting just blocks away from his
front door the entirety of his life. The real stunner, though,
came after dinner, when the massive group set out on its daily
pilgrimage westward through the Village. They migrated down
Broadway, passing the garish stores lined chockablock along
the street, picking their way through the NYU students and
tourist shoppers that the outlets target. They turned onto the
winding West Fourth Street, which flows past Washington
Square Park, then dumps out at the eastern edge of Christopher,
where the group headed on down the famed gay boulevard onto

the pier. There, Justin discovered an oasis. And almost every day throughout the rest of his adolescence he'd go hide out there, arriving around three in the afternoon and staying until as late as three in the morning. "I had no idea!" he exclaims, still gushing at the memory of his discovery. "No idea that there was this 'gay mecca.' I knew there was a gay presence in New York City, but it didn't occur to me there was an area of the city that was like ... *that*."

Every significant event of Justin's subsequent youth occurred in and around the pier. It's where he met his boyfriend— Jamal, a Harvey Milk student who lived with his aunt in East New York—through a mutual friend from Hetrick-Martin. It's where the boys hung out and fell in love. It's where they had fights and broke up and got back together and generally nursed a relationship that would last seven years. It's where Justin accepted his beau's fanciful marriage proposal. And it's where they made love. The pier was divided into two sections. The strip that ran parallel to the West Street highway was the parlor room, where everybody sat around talking and dancing and listening to music. The long, narrow extension that jutted out into the Hudson River and thus offered more privacy was the bedroom, where gay men still secreted off to have sex as late as the 1990s. The youth, who usually had nowhere else to go, hooked up to one side; the adults stayed to the other; community groups parked vans along the highway and handed out condoms and safer-sex info to young and old alike. So for Justin and his boyfriend, the pier was everything from a lover's lane to a sitting room to a nightclub, depending on the hour and the need.

Justin had been bullied at school his whole life, and once he'd found this nirvana at the end of Christopher, subjecting himself to the torment of school seemed more intolerable and less sensible than ever. By fifteen he'd dropped out. "That way I could be waiting outside Harvey Milk for Jamal every day, right when he got out!" Justin quips. But the dropping out and spending all hours of the night at the pier further strained his fraying relationship with his parents, and their rows would prompt recurring episodes of him running away.

Each time he'd storm out of the apartment he'd launch into a brief but increasingly familiar logistical juggling act. He knew he couldn't stay with Jamal at his aunt's place out in East New York, and he was a bit afraid of the neighborhood anyway. But he could couch surf with other friends or, when he couldn't find a welcoming sofa, sleep under the benches in Washington Square Park, on top of the subway grates to leach the system's heat. He'd bounce around like that for a couple of weeks before running out of steam and then come groveling home to his parents. "I'd claim that I was gonna start following the rules," he says, smirking. But soon he'd be back out lingering on the pier all night and arguing with his parents and the cycle would start all over.

These sporadic bouts of homelessness went on until Justin was eighteen, when he finally developed a plan for stabilizing his rocky housing situation: he and Jamal moved into an apartment in the Bronx with Justin's best friend, subletting from her aunt. And it worked out for a while. The three of them scratched and clawed and managed to hold on to the apartment for seven months before the bottom fell out.

Justin had taken classes to earn his high school equivalency, and had just enrolled in community college when he and Jamal moved to the Bronx. But going to school and paying the bills at the same time was too much to handle, and eventually he dropped out in order to work more hours. "Which was a mistake," he says now, explaining that he mortgaged a future he's still trying to rebuild in a futile effort to preserve something none of them had the wherewithal to sustain. "We started being behind on the rent. And the electricity. And the cable." All of which were in his friend's aunt's name, and when the lease ran out she refused to resign; the building owner wouldn't even consider the idea of putting a lease in one of their names, though Jamal was technically no longer a minor.

Justin tried going back home, but his mom had had enough of his coming and going. You keep leaving, she said, so this time, stay gone. The family had just a one-bedroom apartment in the first place, with a walk-in closet big enough to double as a tiny bedroom for either Justin or his younger sister. It had always been a tight space and they'd all gotten used to having one less body to work around, especially his sister, who wasn't about to make room for her brother's defeated return once again. So Justin turned to Green Chimneys. "It was a depressing time in my life. I was just feeling really bad about myself," he says, explaining why, after moving into the Harlem group-apartment with Julius, he sequestered himself in his room and started doing coke every night. It was a drug he'd first tried way back when he was sixteen, and he had never before felt any urge to abuse it. But things had changed, and what was once a playful high became a desperately needed distraction. "It would put me in a trance. I would be in my room with my music and my computer and I'd just be in my own little world."

Julius was never one for the hard stuff. He stuck to pot and booze and he couldn't tolerate having some loner hiding away in his apartment. So he did everything he could to interrupt Justin's nightly routine. "He was always trying to get me to do something with them. Like, 'Let's go here.' Or, 'Let's be creative.'" And the best way to be creative, as far as Julius and the others in the apartment were concerned, was to throw a party as an excuse to decorate the joint. "We'd start hanging arms from mannequins on the walls!" Justin laughs as he recalls the tripped-out designs they'd come up with for the place under Julius's leadership. "We'd still smoke together. We'd party together. But he made it more fun. He made me be around other people and not just by myself. And he was really good about relationship stuff. I would talk to him about Jamal a lot."

It was, after all, a time when Julius was himself in a relationship that he looks back on as particularly healthy. Justin wasn't the only person he was helping out. He'd taken a job at a service organization as a peer counselor for other young black and Latino queers. He was leading safer-sex workshops and talking to people about how to make those often tricky choices about when to be vulnerable and when to protect yourself, and getting paid for all of it—which eliminated the need to do sex work. "I was in a healthy place, and that's the big difference between now and then: the state of mind," Julius says in remembering those halcyon years. He recounts it all like a far-off time that happened to someone else. "I was experiencing my sexuality in its full depth. I was an advocate for condoms. I didn't smoke cigarettes. Weed? Yeah, but not like I do now."

The parties he and Justin and their roommates threw were barn burners, though, and they were in blatant violation of the rules for staying in the Green Chimneys apartment. "We were not supposed to have people over the house after eleven," Justin acknowledges as he recounts the litany of regulations they flouted. "We were not supposed to be drinking in the apartment. We were not supposed to be smoking in the apartment, even cigarettes. All this and more went on, with like fifty people. Banging parties. Music blasting out the windows, and just insanity." They never got caught red-handed, but Justin suspects the administrators knew, since they all eventually got kicked out based on far more minor violations. He was the first one tossed, for missing too many appointments with his counselor.

Julius eventually followed. And that was the beginning of the spiraling emotional free fall he'd already accepted by the time we met. He knew things had gone wrong, and talked about it incessantly. Friends now say that, for all his talk, if Julius was any more out of control than in the past he hid it well. Still, he couldn't escape the feeling. "Everything I've been doing has just been extreme. And I know it's been extreme, so I've distanced myself from a lot of things I used to do."

He certainly traveled a long way from helping Justin and others build healthy relationships.

Julius only has to go about a mile from Crystal Street to meet Tony, but Tony doesn't know that, of course, since Julius would never tell one of his fuck buddies something as personal as his address. He's just returned from clubbing in Manhattan and it's three in the morning, so everyone else in the house is asleep. He'd gone down to the basement to check his e-mail and there was a message from this Tony guy, someone who must have seen him on Adam4Adam during his preparty cybering, so he'd logged in to the site to check the guy out. Tony happened to be there, too.

Like any kind of flirting, online hookups involve an elaborate dance of deciding how much of yourself to reveal and when to do it. The technology aids the process, allowing you to post public and private photos and descriptions; unlocking your private picture to reveal either your unclothed body or your face—depending on which one you've chosen for your public presentation—is the cyber equivalent of offering to buy someone a drink. Julius saw Tony and unlocked himself. Tony responded in kind. "Oh-my-God!" was all Julius could muster when he looked at the picture of Tony's rock-solid frame. "No question about it," Julius had said, "I wanna chow you down!"

It's quite late, however, and even though Tony's house is on one of the neighborhood's tonier blocks, Julius doesn't like walking through East New York at this hour. He'll need to get a ride, he tells Tony, but he'll be there soon.

Yellow cabs don't venture into inner Brooklyn, certainly not to tool around looking for a fare, so limo services fill the economic void. Julius calls the service that works his area, and hops into the standard late-model sedan that shows up to ferry him the ten-minute drive to Tony's place. They pull up in front of the well-kept white house, and Julius pays the six bucks and hops out. The house has been chopped up into rental units, and he bounds up the steps to buzz Tony's apartment number, anxious to get off the nerve-wracking street and in to meet this stranger.

When Tony answers the door, his big, hyper pit bull jumps up and begs for Julius to play with him. That finally puts him at ease, because it's a gorgeous and sweet dog, which is a good sign about Tony's demeanor.

"Hi, I'm Julius."

"I'm Tony."

They nod. Julius smiles.

"You want a drink?"

Julius has already smoked a lot of pot, so he sticks to water as they talk. Tony tells him he's from Panama, that he's in his late twenties, that his dog's name is Mamie, after his mom. He says he's a construction worker, which Julius figures explains the guy's brick-house of a body and titillates his imagination. This is it, Julius thinks, just the kind of "sexy black man" he's been itching to meet. And when the small talk stops and they finally get to the point, the sex is plain amazing.

Julius is hooked. They meet up three times that week alone, and that bothers him. What's he doing? Why's he sweating this guy? Because he's perfect, that's why, at least outwardly. He doesn't really know anything about Tony beyond his sexy vibe, but he figures this is nonetheless the sort of thing that could lead to a connection. "So to prevent myself from doing that, BAM"—he snaps his fingers in a loud pop—"I cut Tony off."

It takes a couple tries. Julius manages to disappear for a few weeks, then suddenly e-mails the guy out of the blue and they'll be fucking again. But it finally stops.

Meanwhile, in all of their intense sexual encounters, neither a condom nor a question about HIV status ever comes up. Not once. Usually Julius will at least hint at it, try to work it into the online conversation by offering up that, as far as he knows, he's HIV-negative. That'll usually prompt the other person to disclose the same and, sometimes, they even negotiate further whether or not to use a condom. Sure, the other guy could be lying, and for that matter Julius can't be sure he hasn't gotten infected since his last test either, given how much unprotected bottoming he does. Still, it's something. With Tony, however, Julius wasn't even thinking about that much. And Tony didn't bring it up either, so why drag things down? "There is a risk. I know there's a risk," he insists. Then he shrugs. He's long since gotten comfortable with risk in his life.

Manny's never seen this guy before. He's a big one, built like a house, with long black hair and a thick accent. He's clearly Italian, so he could be from Bensonhurst, but it sounds more like he's actually recently come all the way from Italy itself. In any case, the guy's newness doesn't really bother Manny. He gets primarily regulars, yeah, but it's not unheard of for random strangers to find their way to Prospect Park. It's a well-known public sex cruising area, always has been, and the men don't just come for the prostitution that takes place over here on the eastern side of the park. To the west, in the area that borders a newly upscale neighborhood known as one of Brooklyn's gay-yuppie enclaves, primarily older white men cruise the woods in search of sex with one another, or with whoever's passing through. Sometimes guys from that end make their way over here, too, bringing a few fresh faces to the otherwise consistent stable of clients. So who knows, maybe that's this guy's story. And more to the point, who cares? It's work. Anyway, he just wants a blow job, so it should be quick and easy.

They situate themselves a little out of the way and the guy assumes the standard position, leaning against a tree, dick out and ready for action.

"I want you to put it in your mouth," he orders, and some-

thing about the way he barks the demand out is, well, demanding. Manny doesn't like it, but again, he thinks, it's work.

"OK," Manny dismissively concedes. "Whatever."

He kneels down in front of the guy and as he's getting situated he pulls out a condom and starts to open it. Rules are rules:
gotta wear condoms when tricking. But the Italian, who's come
with his own rules, doesn't like the idea of this condom stuff and
he says as much. He's in charge here, it's his money, and he's
not buying a blow job through a rubber.

"Just put it in your mouth," he again orders.

Manny looks up and tries to explain that this is the deal, that
he only does it with condoms. He's not really sure how to handle the situation because he's never had any trouble before, not
with the condoms or with any other aspect of the work. It's usually an entirely congenial process, one in which he's largely in
the driver's seat by virtue of his now months' worth of experience working these woods. So even when guys complain about
the condoms, they're not insistent about it. They're often far
more nervous than he is and he's thus able to get his way on all
kinds of things; they're certainly never as belligerent and bossy
as this guy.

He's holding the Italian's penis near his mouth and wondering what to do when he suddenly feels a hand grabbing the
back of his head, gripping down like it's a ball and shoving his
face forward. Instinctually he lets the guy's penis into his mouth
and starts trying to suck, to bring some normalcy to the event,
even as the man keeps uncomfortably forcing it farther and farther in. That's when Manny's old rage once again takes over: the
blinding colors flashing before his eyes and the subsequent
blackened vision, the ringing ears, the same uncontrolled eruption that sent him railing at his seventh-grade sex-ed teacher. He
remembers the knife.

He quickly reaches into his pocket, yanks the knife out, and
flips it open. It's got a serrated edge, perfect for cutting. He

looks up at the guy, and something about the sight of him en-
rages Manny even further. He's somehow actually gotten turned
on by this and has closed his eyes and rolled his head back. He's
not even paying attention to me, Manny thinks. It's like I'm not
even here.

But he is there, and so is his knife.

He brings the jagged blade up to the top edge of the guy's
penis and cuts him, slashing far enough into the flesh for blood
to start gushing out before the guy realizes what's happening.
When he does, he belts out a shout that shatters the woods'
furtive buzz. "He's trying to pull his dick out, but at this point I
clamp down, and he's just screaming," Manny matter-of-factly
recalls. "The worst scream you could hear out of anybody. A
bloodcurdling scream."

Jason runs up and sees Manny's face now full of what he assumes is his own blood, and he pounces on the Italian. He puts
the guy in a headlock and all three of them come crashing into
the dirt and grass. But the Italian's much bigger than either teen
and no doubt raging with adrenaline. He jams a thick elbow
into Jason's gut that fully disables the boy and ends the fight, allowing him to gather himself and stumble out of the park, pre-
sumably to a hospital and not the cops, given the circumstances
of the wound. Manny, who has risen back up to his knees, face
bloodied and clutching his knife, tumbles over and breaks out
in tears. Jason curls into a ball and grips his stomach to fend off
shooting pain from the blow. Recounting the assault turned
stabbing, Manny still feels the dazed aftermath. "We're just kind
of there. Just kind of lying there." He doesn't know how long
they lay there for, but he eventually got up and stumbled out of
the park and down toward Eastern Parkway, face still covered in
blood and eyes glazed over. "I was in a complete daze. I'm sure
I looked ridiculous."

The next morning Jason comes up to Manny and Cassandra's apartment to find his boy still in a funk. He's brought the

knife, which Manny had just left laying on the ground, and the guy's wallet, which Manny had apparently pickpocketed at some point during the fracas. Turns out there's only forty bucks in there, which adds insult to injury because it means the guy hadn't planned on paying full price one way or the other.

Jason feels bad. His caretaker instincts are colliding with his problem-solving skills for dealing with the demands of addiction, and he now regrets ever introducing Manny to the park hustle. He's trying to apologize for it, but Manny's affecting an unconvincing nonchalant posture about the whole thing. "Well, we have money," he reminds Jason. "And that's all that matters."

It's not nearly true, of course. They take a short break and when they return to the work Manny can no longer remember the mental and emotional equation that let it all make sense before the assault. For one, he is on a hair trigger, ready to whip out his knife at every turn, seeing a potential rape in every trick. But he's also lost patience with his regular customers, particularly the ones that used to seem so harmless and quirky. Their fetishes cease to be interesting, if bizarre, experiments and become an affront. It's still not sex per se, but it's also not something he cares to be involved in. The same things they'd always asked for—telling him not just what to do, for instance, but what to say while he does it—are all suddenly disgusting. "Why the fuck you want me to do that?!" he'd testily snap when given his script. "They'd be like, 'Dude, get the fuck out of my face.'" They had decidedly not come to Prospect Park at midnight to have their fantasies questioned and critiqued. The gig was up, and Manny was smart enough to know it. He went back a few times, but that was it. He'd have to find another way to underwrite his queer life—either that or, like Julius, reshape it altogether.

EIGHT

Tenth grade's a new year and Manny's trying to be a new man in it. Or at least he's trying to give school another chance to prove its worth. It's tedious, but it also gives him a welcome opportunity to strut around as "the big man on campus," flaunting his increasingly encyclopedic knowledge of world events. When they discuss Gandhi in class he's able to broaden the conversation from a warm-fuzzy look at nonviolent resistance to talking about worldwide colonialism and India's place in developing-world independence movements. On culture and literature, he's got the advantage of years spent sniffing around the Manhattan avant-garde art scene with Christian, and he can elevate any discussion to the obscure and modern in a way that not even his teachers can keep up with. That's a trick he uses a lot: he remains loath to let the elements of his still-divided lives mix, but he can't resist bringing just enough of one walled-off world into the others to set himself above and apart from the milieu, to spin the outsider label he's internalized into an advantage rather than an embarrassment. So he'll sit with Lisa at their favorite café off lower Manhattan's Union Square—one of the many city spots where New York high schoolers amass in the late afternoons, transforming the daily bustle of shoppers and diners and office workers into a giant public playground— and as the two talk Manny will sprinkle conversation with tales of his exploits with Jason, wowing Lisa with his rebel's life. Then he'll wander down into the East Village to hit some of the galleries and other spots where he knows he'll find Christian's old friends; there, he impresses them with his precociousness, with his ability to mix in like he's a twenty-something despite the fact that he's a teenager. He's also discovered James Baldwin by now and begun to intellectualize the black gay experience, so at the YES program or in Prospect Park he'll sometimes flaunt his privileged education. He may not be able to keep up with his would-be peers' creative self-expression, but he can talk about why it's an important part of identity formation.

All of this misdirection gives him a little breathing room, lets him step back from everybody and try to figure out where he's going. One place he's increasingly clear he's not headed is into the future with Jason. Their relationship has lost a lot of its luster since the assault in the park; and if he's honest with himself, Manny acknowledges it had been tarnished for a while even before that. Jason is happy to live in the moment, even insistent upon it, and Manny is just not that kind of kid. Part of what makes him a voracious reader is his active fantasy life. He's always dreaming up new worlds for himself and for his future, and while few of them involve more of this incessant droning on of school, they do include big things, require big changes. And Jason's not about change. He rarely thinks beyond the immediate next step and what that'll require. That's why Manny's been slowly distancing himself, and it's part of why he's giving school another chance too. "I was just like, OK, there are other things in this world than Jason."

So here he sits in Cassandra's apartment, trying to plow through the dull homework assignment for tomorrow. When the phone rings he knows it's Jason, and he's really not in the mood.

"Hey, can you come down?"

"Not right now. I'm doing homework."

It's certainly a bizarre thing to say. His educational revival aside, the idea that Manny could be so engrossed in his school-work that he wouldn't stop and see what Jason wants is absurd. When has he ever taken school that seriously? Manny knows Jason can see through this ploy and realizes he's being a bit hurtful, but that doesn't change the fact that he just needs space.

"I need help with something, can't you come down?"

"In a while."

"OK," Jason surrenders, sounding wounded. They hang up and Manny goes back to his work.

He's still in love, no question. He still smiles at memories like the time he decided on impulse to forgo a pack of cigarettes in order to buy some flowers for Jason at the Key Food over in the yuppie neighborhood west of the park. He'd been thinking more about the act of buying the flowers than the aesthetics of the stems and buds themselves, so once he had the bouquet he just shoved it in his bag as he left the store. By the time he'd made his way back to Eastern Parkway the flowers were pretty raggedy.

The boys used to be able to laugh at fumbled romantic efforts like that; the misfire made it all the more endearing. But those sorts of moments are less and less common with Jason these days. "I wouldn't say he was thrilled to be alive," Manny says in looking back. By summer's end Jason had lost interest in going out and running around to parties or to the pier, unless it was to find coke or to work the park. His passion for music had even dissipated, which was particularly frustrating to Manny. "He wasn't really concerned about—anything. Except having sex and, I mean, if anything came between us and getting drugs, then all of a sudden he would light up with initiative."

Manny finishes his homework and, figuring he's left poor Jason in limbo long enough, sets out to check up on the guy. It's the beginning of an all-too-familiar ritual. With Cassandra sleeping and Jason's parents out working, he figures they'll sit up all hours of the night doing nothing, or maybe they'll get high and he won't make it to school after all. He goes downstairs, walks up to Jason's door, and lets himself in.

He'd never been fond of the way Jason's parents decorated the place, particularly the carpet. They had put down a huge, long-haired shag carpet, not quite wall to wall but enough to dominate the living room. It was an ugly shade of green, but as Manny turns out of the foyer and walks through the opening leading into the living room, the first thing he notices is that the carpet is black. Then he sees Jason's body sprawled out in the middle of the thick, dark gook and his first response is an audible chuckle, a reaction that still makes him shudder. "I was like, 'What the fuck am I looking at?!'" he offers by way of explanation. "I just had no concept of it. And it was hard to like—" He pauses, still stuck on the detail of the blood. "It really looked black. It didn't look red, in the way that I would have associated blood with, just *black*. It sort of looked sci-fi-ey. And I didn't know what I was looking at, so it took a minute for it to register that he had slit his wrist."

Once reality finally sinks in, he still doesn't know what to do about it. He runs over and starts trying CPR, because he figures that's what you're supposed to do when someone's dying. Except Manny has no idea how to actually do CPR, and he just starts pounding on Jason's chest, manically re-creating what he's seen on television. He never gets to the part where he's supposed to start blowing air into Jason's mouth, because as he pounds his chest a foamy fluid spurts up. That freaks Manny out and, finally, jars him into focus: Call 911, he thinks. Get it together and call 911.

"There's this kind of fear, that I've never experienced again. And it's not as if somebody's going to kill you. I went in there, and it's like you've seen something that you should not see. And, I don't know what you're afraid of, but you just have to get out."

As he's describing the fear to me years later, it strikes him for the first time that, despite the fact that he was standing next to a bloodied body late at night and with no one else around, it never occurred to him to be scared that someone else might be in the apartment, that some third party may have done Jason harm and may still be lingering around, poised to do him harm as well. "It never crossed my mind that somebody had killed him. It was immediately clear to me that he had killed himself. People asked me, over and over, 'Did you see any signs?' And I was just like, 'No,'" he explains. The closest thing to a warning was their phone conversation earlier that night. But he hadn't needed signs to know about Jason's potential for self-annihilation.

Manny is waiting in the building entranceway when the paramedics and cops show up. That strange fear had made him flee, repulsed him back away from Jason, out the door and into the hallway. Jason's apartment sits off to one side, just past the building's front doors, and a large, fake fireplace mantel stands along the far wall. Manny's taken up his perch there.

Just showing the paramedics the body is a trial. New York City EMS walk into enough bloody scenes to know which ones they can fix and which ones are just a matter of going through the motions and getting in touch with the coroner, and the finality with which they go about their business in the apartment is too much for Manny. He prefers waiting outside, slumped against the mantel and numbly watching as the building becomes a crime scene, complete with the public spectacle of neighbors filing out and circling around him. He listens as they talk about him in the third person like he's not standing there, speculating about what happened, wondering what kind of trouble those two boys have gotten themselves into. "He was on drugs, you know," one person points out.

After calling 911, Manny had also called Jason's mom at her

job. The task was all the more difficult because he knew she never liked him, nor had Jason's dad. It wasn't that they were ever mean to him, and in fact they'd been a big help during the whole nightmare of Christian's death and his family cutting Manny out. They had even helped pay for a lawyer over in London to see about getting his stuff back and learn what, if anything, he was entitled to in the way of inheritance. The case went nowhere, since legally Manny and Christian were strangers, but Jason's folks had been truly supportive of their son's best friend. Manny would argue that they actually offered more help than Cassandra mustered. But these flashes of kindness and their overall civility aside, they'd still always made it clear that they weren't at all comfortable with the way he and Jason palled around and cavorted in the streets at all hours of the night. They knew their son was no angel, certainly, and Jason proved time and again that there was no way to blame Manny or anyone else for his troubles. But the two had just as clearly reinforced one another's behavior, so his mom didn't like them hanging around together so much. Plus, she must have felt like there was something about their relationship that wasn't right.

As far as Manny knows, Jason never came out to his parents. He thought of himself as gay by the time he took his life, but not in the way that Manny did. It wasn't an identity for him and thus wasn't something that felt so essential he had to share it with his parents. Still, he and his dad would have awful fights, and listening to Jason's retelling of the often-physical arguments, Manny could always see that Jason's increasingly obvious homosexuality was an undertow. After the suicide, Jason's twin brother, who lived with his grandparents, returned to the apartment, and through conversations with him and his cousins Manny figured out that Jason and his father had been in one of those fights the day he died. One story had it that Jason had finally challenged his father directly by admitting he was homosexual, and that the man had responded by hitting him with an iron.

Whatever actually happened in the hours before Manny walked into that apartment, Jason had likely been calling him earlier that night because he needed to talk about it. That's an uncomfortable truth, but one that Manny insists didn't make him feel guilty then and doesn't now. He instead placed the blame squarely in the hands of Jason's parents, particularly his dad. Jason's parents, in turn, felt the same way about Manny.

Manny's still dazed, leaning on the hallway mantelpiece, when Jason's mom comes storming through the doors. She looks at him with wild rage, but says nothing, just flies past the crowd that's assembling in the entryway and runs into the apartment. Moments later, the detectives show up to take over and direct the first responders at the scene. They talk to Jason's mother first, but the questioning lasts just about fifteen minutes before they're back out in the hallway looking for Manny. "She's obviously been like, 'You need to talk to that faggot because he did this,'" Manny charges, his voice still thick with anger at the woman. "That's obviously the spin she put on it, 'cause the way they carted me back in there—it was something I now recognize as a tactic."

One of the detectives, a tall, built white guy, comes out into the hallway and walks up to Manny.

"Can you come inside?" he asks, politely but firmly, in the way someone does when thinly masking a demand with a question.

"Um, OK."

All of Manny's usual public swagger and outward self-assurance is gone now. He walks obediently and unquestioningly behind the detective, speaks only when spoken to and then only in quiet tones. They walk into the apartment and the detective picks up a chair. He carries it over to the opening between the apartment's foyer and the living room, where Jason's body is still lying in the pool of black sludge.

"Could you just sit there for a second?" the cop says, motioning Manny onto the chair before walking away to talk with his colleagues around the crime scene. The chair is situated so the body is just on the edge of Manny's sight line.

As he sits and waits it's not the body that bothers him, though. He's instead overwhelmed with what he figures to be the smell of blood. The paramedics and the cops have been fussing around in it, he guesses, and that's kicking the smell up into the air. Whether real or imagined, the stench shocks his senses and he feels his stomach start to churn. He thinks he's going to throw up and leans over, but all he gets are dry heaves, and he sits in the chair gagging for a few minutes before he decides he's just got to get out of there. He figures he'll find that cop and ask to be let go, but as he sits up he looks over his shoulder and finds the detective standing right behind him. How long has he just been standing there doing nothing, he wonders?

"Do I have to sit here?" he asks, pleading for a reprieve.

"Well, you know we have a couple of questions," the detective begins. "You were the last person here, before—"

"Well I don't know if I was," Manny interrupts, suddenly getting where this is going and panicking. "Maybe somebody else was here before I found him."

"Oh, OK. Did you guys have an argument?"

"What?"

"You're his best friend, right?"

Manny's now both sick and confused. What's this guy want from him? And what has Jason's mom said? He answers as honestly as he can. "Um, I guess, yeah."

"So did you guys have an argument?"

"No," Manny says, and starts nevertheless detailing their tense exchange earlier in the night—the phone call, Jason mentioning he needed help, his refusal to come down until he finished his homework.

"Help? What kind of help? You don't go help your friends out when they ask?"

It has now been about an hour since Manny first found Jason, and he's held it together as long as he can. Guilty or not, the questions about what went down between them that night are just too much to handle, and he begins to cry. It's one of the few times in Manny's youth when, once backed into an emotional corner, he does not transform his grief or his pain or his fear into rage but, rather, just cries.

The detective asks him a few more questions, pinning down the details of what he saw and how he responded, then sends him out. Manny walks back into the hallway and, rather than going upstairs to wake Cassandra, resumes his post slumped on the floor in front of the mantelpiece. He's not really thinking, not really doing anything but sitting there absorbing the gawks and overheard remarks until, finally, they bring Jason's body out.

A few days later Manny gathers up the strength to go down to see Jason's parents. He's got stuff down there he wants to retrieve, but he's also wondering what's going on with Jason's funeral. Wants to know how he can help, maybe. He knocks on the door and Jason's mom answers.

"Hi, I left some stuff here and I was just wondering if I could get it."

She looks at him and he sees the same searing anger and bubbling hatred he saw the night Jason died, only this time she has no crisis to run off to, no son's body to go see, and she instead stares him down and unloads.

"You do not come back here! You do not call here!"

Manny listens and takes it without mouthing off, without shouting back or tossing the implied accusation back in her face. Indeed, something about it doesn't even quite register with him, because despite the unqualified rebuff he still quietly pushes forward.

"OK, but when's the funeral?"

"It's not happening," she shoots back before slamming the door.

. . .

Despite being up all night the evening Jason died, Manny still dragged himself to school the next day, and actually got there not too long after the day had started. Even given his renewed efforts at school, this was a remarkable fact. School had never been a place he turned to for comfort, but something drew him there that morning. Maybe he just needed to be around people, or maybe he hoped he would stumble into support there, support he no longer even assumed he could get from Cassandra, especially on something involving his love affair with Jason. So he went to school and got there in time for the start of global studies class, where he knew he'd at least find Lisa.

He walked in and sat next to her in the back of the room. He didn't wait to drop the news, and he leaned over as he spoke, hoping to keep it between the two of them.

"Jason killed himself last night."

Lisa opened her mouth and gasped loud enough to shatter his dreams of a clandestine conversation. "I didn't know a human being could take in so much air," he jokes about it in retrospect. "And of course now everyone is looking, and I'm like, great."

So he took the stage and began sketching out the broad picture of what had happened the night before. As he talked, he watched Lisa's face contort with empathetic pain, with the first genuine expression of concern for *his* well-being that he'd come across, and he again became overwhelmed. He didn't make it through the story before he started crying.

He'd lean on Lisa like that for months, turning to her for the sort of support he'd neither been offered nor gone in search of previously. And as they moved through his grief they stumbled on a series of other, more complicated emotions too. There was the sense of abandonment and betrayal. How could Jason do this, he'd ask? How could he do something like that so soon after Christian had died? There was the eventual reciprocated anger at Jason's parents for their presumed abusiveness. And then, most uncomfortably but also most profoundly, there was relief.

"I was crying and I was a mess. But there was a part of me that was really relieved. I remember having the thought, even the next day, that was like, 'You know, maybe I can do something else now.'" And in fact, he stopped doing coke the day Jason died, in part because he couldn't bring himself to seek out the mutual friends he could get it from. He'd already wanted something new, and Jason's death, painful though it may have been, gave him the chance. Maybe, he thought, I can take a break from this.

Of all the heightened risks that Robert Garofalo's 1998 research established for gay kids, none stood out more starkly than suicide. His examination of the Massachusetts data found gay, lesbian, bisexual, and transgender youth to be more than three times as likely as their straight counterparts to report having attempted suicide sometime in the previous year. But that was just the capstone on a decade-long series of studies establishing the fact, dating back to a landmark 1989 federal study that found gay youth to be two to three times more likely to commit suicide—a study that conservative social movement activists protested vociferously, convincing the White House to repudiate its findings. One suicide study after another followed throughout the 1990s, locking in the idea that gay youth find the struggle of their existence to be more painful than it's worth at rates anywhere from two to seven times their straight peers. In a 2001 Pennsylvania State University study that looked at gay, lesbian, and bisexual suicide in the U.S., Canada, and New Zealand, researchers found that one in four gay youth said they'd attempted suicide by the time they turned sixteen. One in ten had done so in the past year, and a third of those made serious enough attempts that they needed emergency care.

The cavalcade of research in the 1990s was in fact so overwhelming that Garofalo told me at the time of his 1998 study that he'd never do another suicide-risk investigation again. For one, he says, these studies overstate our ability to quantify something as slippery as the emotions underlying suicidal behavior, whether it be an actual suicide attempt or the depression and mental health problems that precede it. But moreover, in its effort to identify emotional and mental health problems, public health research has failed to examine the far more compelling and urgent question of solutions. "Most gay youth do not commit suicide," Garofalo points out. "And the thing for me is to begin to figure out what are the factors that put some of these kids at risk, and what are the factors that protect some of them." Or, given all that young people like Manny and Jason face, what we must ask is not how often they give up, but how they manage to survive.

For Carlos, at twenty-one he felt like he was finally starting to move past just surviving in East New York and into real living, to navigating life in the easy way everybody around him seemed able to do. That salvation was coming through his relationship with Ricky. Part of his cyber-boyfriend's magic was that he lived in Orlando, a thousand safe miles away from East New York and the delicate balancing act of Carlos's offline life. If the straight chat sites Carlos had played around in doing cyberdrag had offered him a safe way to explore his physical desires, Ricky offered a similarly nonthreatening outlet for the emotional ones. Their furtive phone calls and their incessant e-mail exchanges built into the most intense nonfamilial connection Carlos had ever had.

Separately, he'd begun talking with his sister-in-law about how to deal with the anxiety attacks he'd always had—the total-system shutdowns that had prompted him to drop out of school, that would abruptly trap him inside the apartment, paralyzed and afraid to so much as go to the store lest he say or do the wrong thing in public. But despite the work he and his sister-in-law were doing, it was still a struggle sorting out all the confusing chaos going on inside his heart and mind. When talking with Ricky he could let some of those inner demons out into the open, where they could be looked at and examined and measured to see just how scary they actually were. The safety of the physical distance between the young men helped make that vulnerability possible for Carlos.

Ricky, on the other hand, sought something more tangible. And as they grew emotionally closer he began to insist that they close their physical distance as well. He wanted to visit Brooklyn.

"You can't!" Carlos would shout, alarmed and desperately trying to stave off Ricky's pleas. "You can't come to my house. I mean, you *can't*."

What would his mom say when this strange guy showed up at their door? And where would he stay if he came to New York? Certainly not with Carlos's family. Moreover, Ricky's turning up in Brooklyn would reveal the elaborate lies he'd been telling everyone about the pretty girl he'd met online and been dating —they all knew far too much about the affair to meet Ricky without figuring out the truth.

Ricky understood all of this. He always knew Carlos wasn't open about being gay with his family or with anyone else, and he'd accepted that untidy fact as their relationship blossomed. But he just couldn't understand why, once they'd fallen in love, that bond didn't trump Carlos's anxieties. He assumed Carlos was playing games with him, that his deep feelings weren't actually as shared as he'd thought. It hurt. For Ricky, Carlos's fear felt more like rejection.

"It wasn't that," Carlos now insists, blowing out the sort of heavy sigh that accompanies regretful memories. "I just couldn't be out. I never even thought of it."

At the time, the whole concept of being "out of the closet" was as strange a concept to Carlos as it had been to Manny when he first stumbled upon his queer identity, something relevant to people Carlos had absolutely nothing to do with. And whatever his feelings for Ricky, they weren't enough to replace his family. To Carlos, that was the choice Ricky was asking him to make, between building their shared love and sustaining the comforting if sometimes stifling love he had in East New York. Sure, maybe Ricky was right, maybe this coming out thing wouldn't be as bad as all that, maybe he could actually have both of his loves. But that wasn't a gamble Carlos could afford to make.

And how could Ricky really get just how much he'd been through with his family, not only throughout their lives but also just in the last year? How could he really understand just how much they all depended on one another as a result?

There was his mom's mental illness, for instance. It became acute about a year before Carlos met Ricky, when she slid into a prolonged schizophrenic episode and had to be hospitalized. "It was frightening to me," Carlos admits. "She was totally different. What was happening to this person I had known my whole life? Sometimes I just left, 'cause it was difficult to see her like that." It grew all the more difficult as everyone's fear turned to frustration and anger. Unable to make sense of what was happening and unable to blame their mother for the chaos her illness was wreaking, they turned on each other. Except Carlos, who turned on himself. "I kind of blamed myself, because I wasn't the best kid. I was going through my own thing, being really rebellious and angry. I didn't know why, but I was that way."

Even though, at the time, he was actually in the middle of an academic renaissance. He'd decided to start trying to make more of his life than just being his parents' son and his siblings' brother. He wanted to get his GED. He'd gone out and picked up the study materials and was committed to the idea. Carlos knew he often got jazzed about new challenges only to peter out down the line and never follow through, and he was determined that wouldn't happen with his GED, even with his mom's illness flaring up.

But then there was the fire.

The adjacent apartment buildings that his whole family called home were dumps; they all knew it and constantly griped about it. Which was a sore point for Carlos. He couldn't stand the way everybody just complained about their living conditions but never actually did anything about the problem. It was always a bunch of bitching and griping and big talk on the front end followed by all the tenants settling for whatever they were given in the end. "I guess my mom didn't think we could do any better," Carlos frets. "The older Puerto Ricans, they're kind of afraid of authority figures, and they don't question. I mean, they'll *complain!* And they'll be heard. But they still don't do anything." Something about that sort of stasis has always irked Carlos—the glacial pace of change in his own life notwithstanding—and he'd actually decided he was going to get out of East New York. Or at least off Gary Avenue. "I didn't want to be like that."

He hadn't expected change to come the way it did, but he nonetheless got his wish to move when the whole lot went up in flames. Both buildings burned out and the family lost nearly everything, including Carlos's GED books. He doesn't know the details of what started the fire, just what happened after it was put out, which was more change than he and his family had ever seen. They were split up and put in shelters around the city. The Red Cross placed him and his mom, who was just starting to recover from her latest bout with schizophrenia, in a hotel that doubled as a temporary shelter in Sheepshead Bay, one of Brooklyn's Atlantic Ocean beach neighborhoods. Carlos remembers the time's high-strung emotions most vividly. "The separation thing was difficult for my mom," he says, "and she cried a lot and didn't know what was gonna happen."

So he knew he had to step up and take care of the two of

them, and it was during this period that he really started to flourish in his role as the family's erstwhile mother figure. He nursed his mom, kept everybody in touch, and navigated the complicated, infuriating city bureaucracy to secure them Section 8 housing back in East New York. The GED plan fell by the wayside, of course, as would many other plans he'd lay for himself in the following years, but his family had needed him and he'd met the challenge. "I spoke well for her and took care of the situation," he explains, nodding proudly to himself.

Ricky couldn't have understood any of this, no matter how clearly Carlos articulated the facts to him. Carlos's family needed him, and he needed them. It was all he'd ever known, most of what he'd ever truly invested anything in. His family was his life, and there was no way he was going to risk his life just to try out being gay. They'd made it too far together.

When most people think about gay youth and the troubles they have with their families, what comes to mind is bald rejection, be it a cold parceling of conditional love or an often-violent casting out like that Jason seems to have faced. And to be sure, that story is all too familiar for young people trying to develop a sexuality that falls outside the bounds of supposed normalcy. But Carlos is hardly alone in facing a different kind of familial problem altogether, and one that is particularly common among gay youth of color. His troubles stem not from his family's push, but its pull.

Conventional wisdom holds that black and Latino America are uniquely homophobic realms; observers look at the central role Bible-thumping preachers and strict Catholic virtues play in black and brown communities and equate them with white evangelicals' hateful messages. But mainstream homophobia in communities of color often comes in a more subtle package, one that happily accommodates gay men and women as long as they subjugate their feelings to those of the larger community.

Our personal and communal histories are replete with examples of homosexual men and women walking the fine line this sexual détente demands—there was Bayard Rustin playing his quiet, behind-the-scenes role as gay adviser to the civil rights movement, alternately embraced and shoved aside depending on how willing he was to keep his widely known homosexuality to himself; Billy Strayhorn anonymously crafting Duke Ellington's swinging hits as he drank himself to an early death at fifty-one; the archetypal gay choir director who's never been seen in public with his partner of twenty years.

And sexuality's not the only thing relegated to the back seat of the bus of racial belonging. Besieged by the range of threats both real and imagined that American life presents to people of color, membership in a larger clan has long offered a crucial buffer upon which survival sometimes quite literally depends, and we jealously guard the organizing identity that binds us. From civil rights to Chicano power, women have chafed as they've labored in movements that have demanded they put their gender second to their race and ethnicity. Up and down the slowly expanding ladder of class in communities of color, people are reminded that the collective's needs are more important than their own. Bill Cosby's much ballyhooed 2004 outburst against what he characterized as self-destructive behavior among low-income blacks was a rare public example of the private dynamic that has long played out along class lines in black America—don't shame us, poor folks are told, you'll tarnish the shine we're trying to put on blackness. The fact that middle-class, straight men are the ones who stand to gain most from this policing of black and brown standards is beside the point; unity has too long been defined as subjugation to a set of racial norms for the gamble of testing the theory to look like a good bet.

We've of course paid dearly for this all-or-nothing allegiance. Communal problems that cry out for solutions go unaddressed

—spousal abuse, mental illness, drug addiction—shied away from for fear that they'll air dirty laundry or just plain be distracting from the grander, unifying agenda. AIDS stands out. Black America's reluctance to address the epidemic, both collectively and individually, has been exhaustively documented, most notably by Cathy Cohen in her book *The Boundaries of Blackness*. That reticence is widely assigned to the homophobia of community leaders, and the trickle-down stigma that drove individuals, gay and straight alike, to avoid taking charge of their sexual health. But here again, it's a unique strain of homophobia: those with the power to shape black public opinion steered clear of AIDS not just because of simple hostility to those most at risk but because they feared drawing blackness close to yet another negative attribute, adding yet another seemingly insurmountable challenge to the already lengthy list.

All of this policing of racial and ethnic identity and belonging seeps down from such big-picture ideas to real lives. The outsize machismo Carlos bumps against troubles him because he knows his full membership in the community depends on his ability to mimic Puerto Rican masculinity, no matter how disingenuous the charade feels. No one had to call him a faggot or punk or *maricón* for him to understand that much. In the end, however, this brand of homophobia is no different from any other; they all hinge on the self-subjugation of gay men and women. Sexual oppression is a particularly corrupting form of bigotry for just that reason—maintaining the closet demands the active consent of those shut within it; the door must be locked from the inside to remain secure.

"If I were to name one of the biggest threats to gay people of color, I'd say it's social isolation," says George Ayala. Time and again, he sees a clear divide between the men he works with who are grounded in some place or some thing to which they feel a genuine belonging, and those who are not. "When gay people of color have a tough time with their families, the challenge is to create their own," Ayala says. "Many of us are doing that successfully. Others are not. And those are the ones who are struggling."

Carlos chose his own closet over Ricky because he needed what modicum of belonging it gave him. He was no different from the community at large in desperately needing a collective buffer against the trauma of growing up poor and Puerto Rican in America, particularly so in a place that has been as ravaged by the deprivations of white racial and economic machinations as East New York. Carl Siciliano, a young, former Catholic monk who founded the Ali Forney Center and has spent years working with gay youth on homelessness and other risk issues, describes the challenge in historically stark terms: as he watches kids from places like East New York move through his shelter —each having given up on Carlos's charade and, as a result, having either pulled up stakes or been pushed out of their neighborhoods and homes—he sees nothing less than refugees. "I think these kids that grow up in that environment have been more hurt and traumatized than any group of people since the Civil War."

To Siciliano and others who have worked with gay youth of color, the question isn't why people like Carlos don't come out, but rather, what is there for them to come out into? And that, Siciliano would argue, is where gay America has failed them as much as the racial and ethnic communities we are more apt to judge. Even for the most resource-independent gay person of color, the broader gay community has done little to counter the unnecessarily polar divide between race and sexuality that haunts Carlos and Manny and others like them. But for those who acutely need the support, financial and otherwise, of the racial and ethnic communities they call home, the singularly white face of mainstream gay America certainly wouldn't appear a safe haven. And it is not. One need not dig deep to find racism in the gay community—drag queens performing in black face,

bars and clubs with unspoken but equally clear racial door policies, white men and women who openly turn black and brown
skin into objects of fetish and revulsion, depending on one's
preferences and moods.

But nor has mainstream gay America been particularly
welcoming for youth in general. Here again, young people
find themselves either objectified or dismissed. And here again,
those who most desperately need help find little. Siciliano will
point out a stat that makes the case all too starkly: researchers
estimate that New York City has anywhere from three thousand
to eight thousand homeless gay youth—the vast majority of
whom have become homeless because of problems surrounding their sexuality at home—yet as of 2006 advocates and the
city's three gay youth shelters had scrounged up enough resources to offer a little over one hundred beds a night in safe,
explicitly gay-affirming housing situations. "Look, I think gay
marriage is an important issue. There are a lot of important issues," Siciliano acknowledges. "But I find it troubling that so
many of our youth are suffering and it's not a priority."

Advocates and service providers working with gay youth all
over the country recite the same list of hurdles to getting other
gay adults involved—lingering trauma from the rabid culture
wars of the '70s and '80s, which stirs up either fears of being
labeled predators or simple reluctance to revisit adolescence, a
time looked upon by many gay adults as a thankfully distant,
painful memory. Garofalo cringes at the response he's seen to
efforts to engage gay adults on youth issues, particularly among
men. His clinic, the Howard Brown Health Center in Chicago,
runs a mentor program pairing gay youth and adults, and the
male mentors report being looked upon skeptically—not by
straight people, but by their gay male peers. "It's, 'Oh, I saw you
hanging out with that young guy,'" Garofalo says of the reaction
mentors report. "I think lesbian, gay, bisexual, and transgender
adults have done a piss-poor job of taking responsibility of the
youth in our community."

All of this conspires to make choices like the one Ricky forced upon Carlos difficult to swallow but easy to make. What he had in East New York wasn't perfect, but it was better than nothing.

Still, sometimes it hurt. I'm a survivor, Carlos would tell himself. I'm here for a reason. But he couldn't always figure out just what that reason was, and he wasn't always satisfied with the answers he got when he studied the question too closely. One day after the fire, after they'd all settled into new apartments back in East New York and Carlos had cemented his role as family linchpin, he turned to his sister and started griping. He'd been having that itch again, that feeling that his static life needed change.

"What am I here for?" he lamented. "I'm really not doing anything 'cause I'm so involved with this family."

"Maybe you're here for us," she posited. She was being sweet but the remark stung.

"That's it?!" he snapped back. "That's all I'm here for, to take care of you guys and deal with your situations? And that's it? What about me?"

NINE

Greenwich Village has been contested space from the start. A village of Lenape Indians lived on the land when, in 1629, the Dutch West India Company decided it could put the area to better use. The company, which ran the New Amsterdam colony south of the area, chased the Lenape off and granted its director, Wouter Van Twiller, two hundred acres of freshly cleared tobacco farmland. The southern border of what was Van Twiller's estate is today's Christopher Street.

Van Twiller feared reprisal attacks from the Lenape he had invaded, so the company created a human buffer by granting the land just south of what is today Christopher to a former slave named Symon Congo. In return for his land and his nominal freedom, Congo was forced to surrender his labor whenever called upon, leave his kids in slavery, and serve as cannon fodder for the Lenape, giving the Dutch time to escape in the event of an attack. But it was the Duke of York, not the Lenape, who would challenge Van Twiller's claim on the space, along with New Amsterdam. In 1664 he kicked the Dutch out and the new owners renamed the area Greenwich.

Greenwich owes its subsequent growth to crime and disease. A series of yellow fever epidemics beginning at the turn of the nineteenth century sent successive waves of New Yorkers north in flight from the presumed miasma of the city and ushered in an era of flourishing development for Greenwich. The state aided that expansion by building Newgate Prison on four acres of land stretching north from Christopher, and in 1794 it attached a set of piers to the end of Christopher in order to bring in prisoners and supplies. Newgate was celebrated at the time as America's first reform-oriented penal institution, in which prisoners were not just warehoused but educated and offered a chance to improve themselves. The bright idea drew not only new Greenwich residents to work in the massive prison, but tourists to visit it, along with a new hotel and affiliated commerce to serve them. Everybody loved this new use of the space —everybody except those held inside the prison, which quickly ballooned from an initial four hundred or so inmates to thousands. Newgate's unhappy and unreformed captives routinely rioted, once burning down most of one wing. The project became untenable and by 1829 the state had sent all the prisoners up to newly built Sing Sing and sold off the land.

Thriving markets grew up in its place, fueled by a series of piers the state built along the Hudson River, turning Greenwich into a bustling port and driving a steady territorial expansion through landfill poured into the Hudson. But as neighborhood historian Stuart Baldwin writes, it was the completion of DeWitt Clinton's Erie Canal in 1825 that sealed the Village's role as "the boiler room of the great ships that would carry America into the 20th century." By connecting the Midwest to the Atlantic Ocean via the Hudson River, the canal put New York's western port at the center of global trade.

Racial tensions would continue to define the contest for ownership of that prosperous space. The white Protestants who dominated the area at the time of the canal's completion did not welcome the Irish and German immigrants who later labored there, and who made up half of the population by midcentury. Those immigrants in turn bitterly shunned the freed slaves who flooded into the area after New York's emancipation. Like everybody else, black New Yorkers came to Greenwich in search of jobs in its thriving industries, but Irish laborers didn't take the potential job competition lightly. In 1863 wartime inflation (along with demagogic politicians) pushed Irish anxieties to the boiling point. A riot that started as a protest against the Union Army's draft turned into a three-day Irish campaign of terror in black neighborhoods—they lynched men and women in the streets, burned businesses employing blacks, even ransacked and burned down a black orphanage.

So it was in keeping with a long tradition of racially tinged competition for this space that, in February of 2002, a group of homeowners posted flyers around the West Village announcing a meeting with the police commissioner, in which residents would implore the Sixth Precinct to finally get tough with the boisterous kids who cavorted en masse around their streets every night. The sponsoring group—dubbed Residents in Distress, or RID, an acronym organizer Jessica Berk said she chose because it matched the name of a popular louse killer—would deny that their complaints had anything to do with the fact that these kids were overwhelmingly black and Latino. Berk and the Community Board, which serves as residents' official voice in city government, said this was strictly a matter of "quality of life"—a term popularized as a raison d'être for the aggressive policing tactics championed by Mayor Rudy Giuliani in the 1990s. Over the years, residents charged, they had been terrorized in their own homes by what one person called "menacing behavior." Community Board chair Aubrey Lees, fresh off a failed run for City Council, said the neighborhood was becoming "a cesspool," soiled with prostitution, drug dealing, public urination, and more. The New York Times breathlessly reported that Berk had even been "slapped by a transvestite." But throughout the subsequent years' long campaign to push the youth out, the West Village resident groups would insist that their complaints had nothing whatsoever to do with sexuality or gender expression, and certainly not race.

Bob Kohler didn't buy it, and he told his neighbors as much.

"They were going to get rid of everything they didn't like that was gay or black or brown," he insists. "I've had people curse me out in meetings for saying it. But of course it's true."

The Sixth Precinct cops are looking askance at sixteen-year-old Manny as he prattles on in a characteristically sarcastic monologue. "My name is Jack *White*," he's intoning. "And *I* am a West Village resident."

It's sort of true, in that he's been crashing on the couch of an older friend who lives in the area for months now; it's one of a handful of makeshift homes he's had since walking out on Cassandra late last fall during the bitter climax of their years' worth of push and pull. But that's not the point. Everybody in the packed room knows the question of actual residence is a proxy for the real dividing line in this battle, and that the sixteen-year-old black kid standing at the mike right now is clearly on the side of what some residents have dubbed "the rowdies," meaning the pier kids. Manny's addressing a crowd of around 150 people, which is a ridiculously large number to show up for a routine community meeting with precinct reps. But that's how things have been down here ever since Berk and the Community Board began haranguing the police into harassing the pier kids. Tense.

Really, ever since September 11 the whole city's been on pins and needles, and the West Village is no different. A simmering conflict between owners of the neighborhood's increasingly sought-after real estate and the pier kids finally erupted into open warfare in late 2001. According to social services providers and Kohler, block patrols and vigilante residents even began targeting the aid workers who came out at night to help the kids —to give HIV tests, to offer counseling or drug-treatment referrals, to pass out condoms or even basic life supplies like toiletries to the homeless ones. Residents would storm up to outreach vans and yell at the workers and volunteers; they got cops to nag them about permits and shoo them along. And at the February 2002 meeting, the police commissioner unveiled the new West Village Initiative. Despite the fact that, according to a *Village Voice* report, all major crimes, from robbery to assault, had dropped 12 percent the year before, and that quality-of-life arrests had gone down 22 percent, this new plan beefed up the number of cops assigned to the Village. Things changed fast after that. Plainclothes officers conducted regular sweeps, locking kids up in batches of as much as a dozen at a time for smoking pot or loitering. One young community organizer who tried to mediate during a sweep along the minihighway that separates the West Side piers and the Village got arrested for obstructing a bicycle path.

But RID and the West Village Initiative came along at a time when changes were also bubbling up among the queer youth in the Village. Grassroots activism had seen a renaissance in New York City. The Giuliani administration's hard-line tactics on everything from policing to welfare services had pushed all kinds of communities to their breaking point, and the 2000 acquittal of four city cops on murder charges in the fatal shooting of unarmed immigrant Amadou Diallo poured fuel on the smoldering fire of dissent. People were looking to get involved in something, for a way to speak up and push back in the way Lionel and Hermone were being stirred in East New York. Amid all of this burgeoning activism, a handful of queer teens who'd been active in a variety of organizations came together with the idea of forming one of their own, to specifically address the needs of gay kids of color like themselves. They named their group Fabulous Independent Educated Radicals for Community Empowerment, or FIERCE!

FIERCE! met at the Neutral Zone, a drop-in center and service organization on the northern edge of the Village that was originally set up at the end of Christopher but which had been pushed out by residents years ago. It wasn't long after FIERCE!

started meeting that the aggressive policing and resident harassment became an overwhelming concern for them. Kids would come running into the drop-in center from Christopher Street, breathless with stories of sweeps that had just gone down or, on the other hand, of cops ignoring their pleas for help when they got pelted with garbage and eggs by residents.

Things got serious one afternoon in the summer of 2001, not long after FIERCE! started meeting. Justin came into the Zone and told a jaw-dropping tale that seemed to crystallize what was going on down on the pier. He and his pals had been on the pier the night before when a kid they'd seen around but didn't really know came racing past in what seemed like a sprint for his life. Seconds later Justin realized it was in fact a matter of life and death, as an older guy well-known as a drug dealer working the area came trucking up close on the kid's heels. Folks could smell violence and, Justin included, they all scurried to get out of the way. Who knew if the guy carried a gun? Nobody wanted to be in the line of fire when shots started popping off. So they darted across the highway and amassed on the other side of the street, watching from afar as the dealer caught up with the kid and stabbed him. Only after the fact did it dawn on Justin and everybody else that the cops who had been constantly hounding them all summer had been nowhere to be found when the fight erupted. They're here ghosting us night and day, Justin fumed as he told the story to a rapt crowd at the Zone, anxiously waiting to pounce on our slightest infraction, but nobody's around to stop this guy from getting stabbed?

FIERCE! realized that just defending this turf, with all of its good and all of its bad, would have to become its priority. At the time, Maya Iwata ran a program that trained the Village youth to be peer counselors for one another, and she was among a group of adults who mentored the FIERCE! group. She remembers the urgency her young charges felt about maintaining the space they'd carved out over the years, and its unique ability to energize the youth in general. "It's very, very hard to find community" as poor, often homeless gay kids of color, Iwata explains. "The piers were a physical place, the Village was a physical place, where you could just *be*—and be yourself." For all the dangers and risks that happened in that place, it nonetheless provided something utterly basic for Iwata's youth, something they had scrambled through often-deadly circumstances to find. "It's just nice to be with a group of people who understand who you are." Kohler, a Neutral Zone board member, adds that the kids also really didn't have much choice about whether to fight for the space. "Sometimes I look around at the piers and I think, 'Where would they be if they didn't have this? Where would they be?' "

So FIERCE! showed up at the Community Board meetings and police forums with several dozen pier kids, demanding to be heard and waving colorful hand-painted signs insisting on their equal claim to this space—"Whose Streets? Our Streets Too!"; "Clean Up Your Streets? We Are NOT Trash!!!"; "Whose Quality of Life?" That's how they got labeled "rowdies." The residents were enraged to find themselves matched in number at meetings they'd meant to be a platform for their own complaints, and they railed at the idea of kids they considered to be outsiders presuming a right to speak at such official proceedings. When they weren't called rowdies, they were shorthanded as "BBQs," for the non-Manhattan neighborhoods they hailed from—Brooklyn, the Bronx, and Queens. As one woman put it in a meeting recounted by the *Village Voice*: "Maybe there should be a way to say, 'You're not welcome here.' The cops used to do that. They'd drive unwanted people to Jersey and dump them."

Which is why Manny is at an April 2002 meeting posing as Jack White, Village resident. The kids are getting a chance to speak at this meeting, since the organizers have set up a microphone in the aisle for questioners to line up at, thereby inadvertently abdicating the moderator's ability to control the conversation like at previous meetings. Manny's taking advantage of the opening and using it to act out, to make a mockery of what he and others see as a farce in the first place. He lives near the bars and clubs frequented by NYU students, he claims, and he's mortified by what he sees. They stumble out of the bars at all hours of the night, stinking drunk, vomiting on the sidewalk, shouting at one another and generally, well, menacing him. And the cops? They do nothing about this indignity he suffers. He wants action. The cops and residents roll their eyes; the FIERCE! kids laugh at his brazenness.

Manny's a relatively new face on the scene. He'd noticed the competing flyers of the residents and FIERCE! a while back, and had stopped by some of the meetings to see what was up. This is the first time he's decided to step up and get into the mix of this particular fight, but he considers himself a seasoned activist these days—and he's indeed seen an unusual amount of muck-raking action for a sixteen-year-old.

Jason's death spurred a lot of change in Manny's life. The following summer, he'd been walking around downtown when he strolled into the office of one of the left-wing protest groups that were planning a rally against U.S. trade and development policies. He signed up and immersed himself in work on the event, which was to be held in Washington, D.C., that fall. It was perfect for him: an organization peopled with engaged, well-read politicos—many of them gay, if white—who genuinely valued his ideas despite his youth and, quite the opposite of school, who affirmed the radicalism he hoped to cultivate. He dove headfirst into the work and filled the hours he once spent snorting coke and turning tricks by working on the campaign's media team, shuttling back and forth to D.C. all summer and generally being a big shot.

And when school finally started back up it never even occurred to him to interrupt the revolution he considered himself to be leading. He wasn't even in the city at the time. The rally was scheduled for September 29, and he and his colleagues on the media team were drowning in preparations down in Washington. So when Cassandra called he didn't mince words.

"When are you coming back?"

"I'm not."

"You're not going to go to school?"

"No. I'm done. I'm gonna do this, Ma," he explained, referring not just to the trade-policy rally itself but to the rabble-rousing and media machinating it involved. He'd found his calling, he said, and he didn't need high school to do it. "I'll get my GED, and isn't that what it's about anyway? That piece of paper?"

He wasn't all that surprised when, by and large, Cassandra didn't give him a hard time about the decision. She'd never seen him so passionate about anything before. And neither of them were obtuse enough to overlook the fact that it was only a matter of time before Manny dropped out of school; the only question was what he'd be doing with his time when he finally quit. Might as well happen while he was focused on something positive, something that might, somehow, get him a future. And also something that involved collecting a paycheck, because Cassandra was clear with her son about one thing: if you're not going to school, you're paying rent.

Fair enough, Manny agreed. Life was too good to fight with Cassandra. He was awash in romance, and not just because he had his new revolutionary lifestyle. He'd also met David. A rail-thin, sixteen-year-old Filipino immigrant, David grew up in a well-off and strictly conservative family in Queens, and as a result he was calling himself straight when he and Manny met working on the rally. Manny knew better. David just asked too many questions, was way too curious about all the ins and outs of Manny's gay life, to actually be a straight boy.

He wasn't Manny's type, physically or stylistically. His jet-black hair and wispy, frail frame were nothing like the thick, beefy bodies that normally caught Manny's eye, and the punk rock image he cultivated was hardly Manny's thing either. The ripped jeans with patches sewn all over the place, the piercings and whatnot, all of that would be an embarrassment back in Brooklyn, he thought. But in the end, the all-encompassing nature of David's own activism turned Manny on way more than the other stuff turned him off. "We were drawn to each other's passion," Manny explains. "He'd been in the activist world a lot longer, so at first he was kind of showing me the ropes of his little anarcho-punk scene, and I was just like, 'This does not apply to me.'" They'd geek out and argue about stuff like that, about race theory and how it shapes progressive social movements and other assorted obscurities. "I mean, we just immediately gravitated to each other."

One day that summer, Manny showed David around the West Village, playing gay tour guide—took him to the Oscar Wilde bookstore, walked him down Christopher, and capped it all off by cornering him into a public make-out session. It was love at first kiss. David dropped the straight act immediately and the two paired off, becoming the gay-teen poster couple of the anti–global trade movement. "We were really cute," Manny brags.

For Manny, this was it. He'd figured life out and found where he belonged. "It was light-years more stable than whatever I had with Jason," he says. "I thought I was so grown. I was like, 'This is a *real* relationship. I'm finally getting my shit together.'"

And as a result he opened himself up to David in ways he hadn't for anybody previously. Outside of the confines of their relationship, he still vigilantly guarded the borders of his boxed-off lives, but between them there were no secrets for Manny, no barriers. He told David everything, told him about the tricking and the drugs, told him about Jason and about the awful circumstances of his suicide. Manny didn't repudiate his time with Jason, and he in fact steadfastly refused to express regret about any of it. But neither was it a time to which he wanted to return. "I wasn't trying to become a different person or distance myself from the kind of person I was," Manny explains of his thinking, then and now. "It was just a different time in my life, but it was *my* life." He still rather sees it all as a queer battle scar, the unfortunate but entirely necessary stage he had to wade through to arrive at the place he is today. His past wasn't cool, he lectured David, but it was real; not everybody grew up rich and closeted in Queens. "I was trying to tell him that gay life wasn't all like Chelsea. There was some real shit." And it's a reality that Manny holds close to this day, that continues to inform the way he moves through the world. His identity is rooted in the near misses of destruction. "I wanted him to know: This is my baggage. This is what I'm coming to the table with."

So he even brought David home to Brooklyn. They'd been at work on a Saturday, having just returned from D.C., and David was going on about how he wanted to bleach his hair—yet another of these punk styles Manny couldn't quite connect with. But it nonetheless presented an opportunity to push the couple-weeks-old relationship further.

"I can bleach your hair," he nonchalantly offered. "Come over."

They left the office that afternoon and took the subway out to Manny and Cassandra's place on Eastern Parkway. Cassandra wasn't there, luckily. So Manny turned on the TV and grabbed a towel. He pulled up a chair and warned David he should take his shirt off, because he didn't want to ruin it, and gave him the towel to wrap around his shoulders. That's when Manny really noticed just how skinny the guy was, and he was surprised when he found it more adorable than anything else.

David sat down and they clicked through the channels while Manny played beautician. Manny loved *Law & Order* reruns, but

David couldn't be bothered with such frivolity as primetime television, or TV of any sort, for that matter. He disdainfully mocked everything about the show the whole way through. "This is so stupid!" he'd jeer. "This would never happen." It was just one more example of the over-it-all air that Manny found so attractive about David—a kindred spirit at last. "He was just so irate all the time, which I just thought was so cute!"

By night's end they found themselves on the couch making out. One thing led to another—or Manny took one thing to the next—and they retreated to the bedroom, where they had sex. It was David's first time, and Manny did his best to make it a careful, intimate experience for them both. They did it more than once that day, with Manny slowly walking David through the process of condoms and lube and anal sex. David trusted him each step of the way, and Manny held that trust dear. That's another reason why he decided to share everything about himself: if David could show that kind of trust, so could he. It was an unusual and revolutionary experience in Manny's young, but full sexual life; it drew them close and held them there.

Things were going well with Cassandra at the time Manny and David fell in love. Part of what was helping the two get along was that they'd largely stopped demanding a mother-son relationship from one another. Cassandra didn't seek too much control, and Manny didn't ask for too much coddling. Instead, they dealt with each other as friends, if not peers. She was still clearly in charge, clearly an authority figure, but they could have frank talks that both found refreshing. They'd often fight as a result of each other's honesty, but these were the kind of arguments that could spur breakthroughs rather than the stagnation bred by their previous silence and avoidance of each other. So it wasn't altogether out of order when Cassandra raised her concerns bluntly the day after she met David, who had been on his way out of her apartment and headed back to Queens after he and Manny made love for the first time. David had seemed like a good kid to her, but she had a bone to pick.

"Did you guys do it?"

Manny wasn't put off by the inquiry, and simply told her that, yes, they had.

"You know, that's not OK," she responded sternly. "I'm not OK with that happening in my house."

They didn't bother to sort out whether it was the gay part or just teenage sex period that bothered her, they just commenced shouting, until Manny stormed off to his room and slammed the door.

But that was just the opening uproar that would make way for their breakthrough. He came back out after they'd both blown off some steam and they sorted it out. "Look," he told her. "I'm gonna have sex. And it's gonna happen either here or somewhere else."

She couldn't argue the point. She had no idea about Manny's onetime exploits in Prospect Park, but she could imagine the trouble a sexually active gay kid could get himself into out on the streets of New York City. Better that it happen in a safe environment.

"Fine," she conceded. "But not while I'm here. I don't want to be hearing that."

And so a deal was struck. And within that détente, they were able to take their relationship places they'd never been.

It helped that Cassandra grew genuinely fond of David. "She loved him," Manny recalls, laughing broadly at one of the few things he and Cassandra saw eye to eye on. "She thought he was the cutest thing in the world." So she welcomed David into their home, and as the boys' relationship progressed he spent more and more time on Eastern Parkway, thankfully far away from Queens and his own parents' intensifying disapproval of the radical-activist life he was building for himself. Unlike Manny, David was still in school—in his senior year—and doing quite well, at that. But his parents correctly suspected he was losing focus, and had begun to ride him about the fact. Cassandra, on the other hand, found the boys' activism exciting, a refreshing change in Manny's level of engagement. She'd shaken some foundations of her own in her younger days, as a participant in the Puerto Rican independence movement, and had even spent time locked up for those exploits. Being around their place affirmed rather than stymied David's ambitions.

David was also decidedly not open to his family about his newfound gayness, and he found the charade he had to keep up there untenable. He preferred hanging out with Manny and Cassandra, the three of them cooking dinner and comfortably palling around, he and Manny's love on full, unapologetic display.

And David's need to hide out at their apartment also drove Manny and Cassandra into long-overdue conversations about his own sexuality. They wouldn't come at the topic head-on, but rather back into it through David's situation. When he wasn't around, Cassandra would take up her social worker posture and wonder aloud about the dynamic between David and his mother; Manny would talk her through how hard it must be for David, as well. She read the self-help classic *Now That You Know: A Parents' Guide to Understanding Their Gay and Lesbian Children*. "I was really impressed with her and how open she was trying to be," Manny says. Then he sighs, raises his eyebrows, and gives up a shrugging nod to what came next in their relationship. "I think she just reached the end of her rope with being open."

By November, Manny and David had been through an awful lot together. Three days after they first made love, New York City was rocked by the attacks on the World Trade Center. They'd both been downtown when the towers came down, and once they managed to find each other in the chaos, they roamed the streets of lower Manhattan in a stupefied daze just like every-body else, David trying to put the medic training he'd just got-ten to some sort of use. He lost two cousins in the attack. Manny lost a friend and neighbor. Since there was no feasible way for David to get back to Queens at the day's end, they walked home to Manny's apartment over the Brooklyn Bridge and held each other that night.

In the wake of the attacks the trade rally they'd been plan-ning suddenly shifted to an antimilitarism march. The contro-versial September 29 demonstration would be one of the first in a series of antiwar rallies that shocked the Western world in the buildup to the Iraq war, and David and Manny worked furi-ously over the few short weeks after 9/11 to reshape the event. Even after the rally was over, they stayed busy with follow-up, and they turned the apartment into a satellite office of the move-ment, working and buzzing around together for twelve, thirteen hours a day.

Nowadays, looking back on the time, Manny suspects Cas-sandra eventually felt left out, like their burgeoning triparty friendship came second to the boys' work. And maybe a bit jeal-ous too, as their work perhaps reminded her of the idealism she'd long since abandoned in favor of a more stable life as a working-class migrant in New York City. He's also since learned that by then her depression had been diagnosed, and she was struggling to maintain a medication regimen. Whatever the cause, sometime in November she decided she'd had enough of David. They were sitting in the apartment, just her and Manny, when she turned to him and said it.

"David is coming over here a lot," she began in an argu-mentative tone.

It was true. David was there three or four evenings a week by this point, rarely spending the night, but nonetheless ever-present. Still, Manny couldn't figure out where Cassandra's sud-den irritation was coming from. Why was she blindsiding him with this bizarre attack? He looked at her as she sat silent for a while, something she often did when stewing with anger. He braced himself for whatever was coming.

"This is not OK," she said, shaking her head. "I can't have these *maricóns* running round the house! What will people say?"

Manny ramped up to meet the challenge. "What did you say?!" he screamed.

"You heard me!" she fired back, then stormed off to her room.

Manny didn't pause. He went straight to his room as well, grabbed two duffel bags and stuffed them with clothes and whatever papers he could think to grab. He gathered up his things and as he headed back into the front room Cassandra confronted him.

"Where are you going?"

"I'm done! I'm leaving."

Cassandra snatched up the house broom, raised it in the air, and ran toward him. If he was leaving, she was going to be throwing him out.

Manny brushed past her largely symbolic attack and stormed out of the apartment, down the stairs and out onto Eastern Parkway. It wasn't until he got out into the night air and found himself standing on the sidewalk alongside the bustling thoroughfare that he stopped to think about where exactly he was going.

He stood there on the dark street utterly confused about what had just unfolded in the apartment above him. It was a disorderliness he'd now spent too many years trying to decipher, and he meant exactly what he'd told Cassandra on his way out the door. He was done with that stage of his life. Despite the winding, pitted path he'd had to travel ever since his preteen physical epiphanies, he felt he'd finally figured out what his sexuality meant for himself. It meant the love he found with David, yes, but it also meant paying a price. This was just what he'd been trying to explain to David in these last, otherwise blissful weeks—love like theirs doesn't come easy or cheap. You could find it, but you had to be willing to do what it takes to live it out, you had to absorb a few battle scars. Jason had taught him that. And Cassandra had just reminded him of the lesson.

By now Manny had developed a formidable network of white adults—some gay, some straight—whom he knew exactly how to impress. Being a precocious black boy had its perks—you could wow opportunities out of white folks with the wit and charm they didn't expect of you. That's what his love for David would cost for now. So he dug out his cell phone and called up a white lesbian couple he knew from working on the rally. They had a nice three-bedroom place not too far away, over in Bed-Stuy. He told them what happened and they of course did their best to talk him into going back upstairs and trying to work things out, but by this point that was out of the question for Manny. She'd called him a faggot. It was deeply insulting and hurtful in and of itself, but it was also in many ways just the last straw. Like high school, he never really expected to last through his teens living with Cassandra; he'd already decided that home no more accommodated his emotional and physical needs than school had met his educational ones. He definitely wasn't going back, and once he'd convinced his coworkers of that fact they told him to come on over.

Manny gathered up his duffel bags once again. He turned and headed down the sprawling boulevard, walking in the opposite direction of not only his mom's apartment but of the well-worn path he and Jason had trod to and from Prospect Park as well. The first block or two he'd have walked under the warm splashes of light that flood the sidewalks near the grand old Brooklyn Museum, a soft glow meant to keep its stately white marble illuminated even at night. Soon thereafter, he'd have plunged into the long dark expanse of Eastern Parkway, trudging along on its seemingly interminable reach into Brooklyn's heart.

Manny's journey was a mercifully short one though. He

schlepped with his duffels in the dark for only a few minutes before he arrived at the same subway entrance that he and Cassandra would have embarked from years before, had she not abruptly dragged him into their new home after visiting the park. He climbed down the stairs onto the outdoor platform and stood waiting for the tiny two-car shuttle train that bridges the relatively small geographic space separating the Prospect Park area attractions and the inner realms of central Brooklyn. From this stop, the train climbs onto an elevated track and rumbles along above a desolate avenue until it dead-ends in Bed-Stuy, where his urban-pioneer coworkers had purchased one of the neighborhood's famous brownstones.

The train arrived and Manny boarded. He'd already explained to himself that this was not a big deal; it was just the natural order of things for his life. He was sixteen, but as far as he was concerned he was now truly grown, and this was the start of his adult life. So he rode peacefully as he traveled the two short stops into homelessness.

TEN

Hermone was sitting in the FIERCE! office when Julius came sashaying in, early in 2003, looking to apply for a spot in the paid training program the group had just announced.

It had now been nearly a year since the fracas over the pier kids' right to space on Christopher Street erupted, and the group had become something of a cause célèbre in the youth social-services world. Manny and others working on the media team had helped to orchestrate a few big splashes for the campaign during 2002, and their careful organizing efforts had drawn the support of lots of allies who were thrilled to connect the youth in their own programs with something more proactive than reactive for once, something that didn't just serve their deficiencies, but rather offered a chance for them to turn the organizational strengths they flaunted in the ball scene toward getting a political voice too.

That's where Hermone was coming from. She'd been in East New York for over a year, and she'd put down rare roots there. The bond between her and Lionel and their other two roommates had grown only deeper as they started finding ways to do just the sort of organizing they'd dreamed up when first moving in. And for once, Hermone got the feeling that she could not only make a connection, but stay put with it. After bouncing around the globe and the country her whole short life, she'd decided Brooklyn was home.

She'd just taken a gig with FIERCE! in late 2002, and was charged with facilitating a process through which the youth members could figure out what their activism was going to be all about. "It's not really about the piers," she'd say. "It's about healing." And in that she had a point. The West Village streets offered an important place to gather, sure, but it wasn't all that safe or supportive a place, and never had been.

It's not just all the risk taking that goes on there, there's something deeper too. It's easy to romanticize the Village streets as pulsating with a peace-and-love vibe, and that's part of it, but it's not always that way. Like anywhere else, not everybody on the Christopher Street pier loves one another, not everything the kids organize is supportive. The competition of the balls often pits the youngest house members against one another in ways that are hardly what one would call healthy. The crowds circling around a voguing competition, whether it be on a grand ball stage or a Village street corner, erupt into the loudest hoots and applause at moves that demean competitors; the result is too often brutal, even deadly, violence between house members. Following one ball during Washington, D.C.'s, gay pride in the late 1990s, a shootout erupted over what was rumored to be a long-standing grudge between voguers in two of the houses known for their rougher edge. In cities with newer ball scenes, where houses are working to establish themselves, vogue competitions regularly erupt into fights. And a disturbing number of the categories in any given ball glorify unattainable wealth and status to the point of fetish; it's not surprising, then, that criminal exploits ranging from petty shoplifting to large-scale credit card fraud grow up out of some houses, as members pursue and obtain symbols of the wealth and status they can't actually possess.

What the young people really needed, Hermone argued, was to locate home and belonging within themselves, to build enough healthy microcommunities that they could take care of one another no matter where they gathered. That's what she had been learning about herself in recent years, and what she was trying to put into practice in her life back at the Crystal Street house in East New York. And as usual, she was bringing that personal into the political of her job at FIERCE! where she hoped to facilitate some of the one-on-one connections that she passionately believes are step one in the healing process. "It's much simpler than people make it out be," she says of organizing and community building. "It's not leading a campaign and this and that and the third. It's locking into somebody. Feeling somebody. Just having the courage to allow somebody in. That's it."

And right away, it looked like she was going to find something special like that with Julius.

Julius came into the office with a white kid who was working hard at being down. FIERCE!'s celebrity status had helped it win a grant to pay stipends to a crop of young people who would go through an extended leadership-training program, and Julius had heard about it. He was standing there trying to talk to Hermone about applying, but the white guy he was with was obviously working his nerves. Something about Hermone seemed to set the kid off-balance, to make him act like he had something to prove. He was carrying on about Hermone's dreads and how he was going to get some of his own and how good they'd look on him. Hermone and Julius kept exchanging knowing and annoyed looks, until Julius finally just cut the kid off.

"Enough, miss thing," he snapped, smiling at Hermone, then turned on his heels to make an exit. "Let's be out." As he switched away, Hermone laughed to herself at his playful self-assertion. They would become fast friends.

It started later that winter as Hermone facilitated weekly meetings in which members gathered at the FIERCE! office

to discuss their collective future. What should this organization's purpose be? How should decisions be made within it?
Julius was a regular in these meetings and a standout in the
leadership-training program, which he'd go on to help direct
in later years. He'd also roll up his sleeves and get involved in
the tedius, arduous process of turning this notion of youth-run,
youth-driven activism in the Village into something more tangible: an actual organization. He'd never shied away from that
kind of labor. He liked putting affairs in order and making sure
all the i's are dotted and all the t's crossed, he'd just rarely had
an outlet for that skill since leaving north Florida and the yearbook club and the assorted extracurriculars he'd poured himself
into there.

As the planning meetings moved along, Hermone also
spent as much time as possible in individual sessions with the
members, nominally to get their candid input on the group's
future but more to just find out what they needed in their lives
and how she and everybody else could help fill that gap. She got
quite close to a number of the members this way, and it wasn't
long before the kids started finding their way to Crystal Street.

"I brought all these people home," she says with a wistful
laugh, as she recounts how the East New York house she and Lionel and their roommates were sharing slowly turned into an
informal emergency-housing shelter for queer youth. They'd
be preparing for one meeting or another and would be in need
of a place to gather; somebody would turn to Hermone. "They
were like, 'Let's go to your house' "—and she'd trip over the nonchalant suggestion. "Um, *Okaaay*," she'd tentatively concede.
"At first I was hesitant."

Hermone was at odds with herself. Having opened up to the
youth and encouraged them to do the same, she now feared
blurring the lines that she thought equally important to maintain. She wasn't a member, she'd tell herself. She didn't share
the kids' life experiences and shouldn't confuse the point. This

was their organization and their world; her role was solely to facilitate them in taking charge of it. And no matter how invigorating she found their personalities, she was at pains not to make the mistake of appropriating their lives for herself in the way that that white kid had wanted to do with her dreads.

In the end, practicality and humanity overtook those sorts of ideological concerns. The kids had begun to see her as a mentor, a mothering big sister of sorts, and they had real-life problems that she couldn't just ignore.

So when one young transgender member got kicked out of his house, Hermone asked Lionel and the others if they could put the guy up for a while. Everybody readily agreed, and that's where it began. Over the winter of 2003 and through the summer, the kids just kept coming, with Julius later joining the migration when he got kicked out of the Harlem apartment.

"The house was fab-u-lous! It was just very gay," Hermone jokes. That was the thing about the kids FIERCE! organized. Their energy resonated not just with Hermone but with everyone who spent time with them. Julius's dichotomous story of big successes and equally big failures is maddeningly unexceptional. So many of the people Hermone met had an awe-inspiring ability to not just make things happen in their lives, but to bring creativity and beauty wherever they went. Yet so much of that capacity had been spent on simple survival. "They're fucking fierce," Hermone gushes in a typically bittersweet riff about the kids. "They're so beautiful, and they're so hurt. They're amazing, strong, brilliant people with a lot of passion for life and intellectual drive and skill and possibility." She pauses to breathe. "And just forced into instability—homelessness, health is a huge issue—just lack of stability. Lack of stable figures in people's lives."

So she did what she could to become a fixture for the ones she connected with at FIERCE! It made sense. This was the role she'd already taken on in the larger work that the four of them were now doing in East New York. At the time Hermone came to FIERCE! she had been particularly interested in working not just with those who had bad things done to them, but with some of the evildoers as well. That grew out of her experiences while leading the women's group on Rikers Island. The young women in her group were overwhelmingly involved in same-gender relationships, both while in and out of lockup, and the stories she heard of the domestic violence they inflicted upon one another were shocking. She developed a thing for conflict mediation, and added that focus to her work in East New York, particularly when all of the "baby dykes" in the neighborhood moved from just coming out to her to confiding their problems and looking to her for help. "They'd call and be like, 'Yo, I just beat up my girlfriend,' " she explains, and she'd be compelled to talk them through the moment. She'd bring the couple together to figure out what scars they were each nursing from previous relationships, romantic and otherwise, and discuss how to stop the abuse before it happened in the future. She'd try to be a stabilizing presence for both parties.

It made sense that Hermone would offer this same openness to the FIERCE! youth as well. And of them all, the one that she'd pour herself most deeply into was Julius. Looking back on it now, she likes to think they did in fact heal each other, and that she helped stabilize him, at least for a time. But Julius had already been through a great deal by the time he tumbled out of his Harlem apartment and landed on Crystal Street. Maybe Lionel puts it best: "Julius, he was too far gone."

In addition to everything else that Julius was feeling after getting kicked out of Green Chimneys and landing in East New York—at Hermone's invite—he had gone back to doing sex work to make the frayed ends of his life meet. He didn't try to hide it, and it wasn't something he was ashamed of, at least not outwardly, though he knew it took a toll. So did Hermone.

She didn't try to make him stop, which wasn't something she had the power to do anyway. That's the sort of choice he'd have to make on his own. But she made herself available however she could to help tamp down the amount of harm the whole exchange would do to him each time. She asked him to tell her whenever he was going out on a call, to give her some idea of where he would be working, and to check in with her when it was over.

The check-ins were intense, but to Hermone they were the point at which healing could occur. The main thing was to have him talk it all out. Julius would come home and they'd set up somewhere in the house—maybe at the long wooden table that centers the colorful kitchen, or in one of the bedrooms if they had that kind of space—and he'd detail everything that went down on the encounter. Hermone was always struck by how much the tricks had unloaded onto him. Julius may have kept strict distances in his own sex life, but he was remarkably open to at least giving his clients the impression of a connection; he sold more than his body to these men. But he was also just a naturally open guy. He could get on easily with people he'd just met, laugh and share with them as if they were old friends. That's what made the closed, distant posture of his personal sexual and would-be dating life so bizarre. Hermone figured he'd just sealed himself off following a particularly bad breakup he'd gone through as he was leaving Harlem, and if pushed to explain it that's what Julius would say, too.

These are the things the two of them would sit and sort out during the rare quiet hours on Crystal Street. On nights when Julius didn't go out, they could be found out on the front stoop with the clutter of Lionel's never-ending renovation projects, the paint buckets and piles of bricks and concrete bags and wood scraps overflowing out of the tiny space under the narrow, painted stairs. Hermone would sit on a stair below Julius, and he'd fuss over her dreads in his unofficial role as her hairdresser. Or they'd be down in the crammed basement, each at a computer terminal writing in their journals and occasionally pausing to share a thought or a feeling. They were drawn to each other's spirituality, shared an appreciation of the nonphysical world and the way it binds folks up.

And in those peaceful interludes Julius would try to explain what was going on with him, how he was coping with what his Green Chimneys social worker had described in a letter to federal investigators of his foster parents as "symptoms of Major Depressive Disorder and Post-traumatic Stress Disorder." He went on to detail Julius's "lack of initiative/motivation . . . needing to be isolated . . . decreased/increased libidinal drives (in extremes)." This last point disturbed Julius the most—understandably, given sexuality's central role in propelling him to New York City in the first place. He couldn't make sense of it.

The way he handled Trevor was particularly bizarre.

Trevor was the one guy Julius met through his Adam4Adam exploits who managed to trip up his comfortably numb stroll. He lived a lot farther away than Julius was usually willing to travel for an online hookup, in his own one-bedroom apartment way over in Flatbush, Brooklyn, which meant hopping not one but two subway transfers and then walking alone down five dark blocks in an unfamiliar neighborhood. Any part of that would normally disqualify a would-be suitor, but there was something about Trevor. He was smart, for instance, studying for his master's in some sort of graphics program at City University. And at twenty-eight, he was enough older than the twenty-one-year-old Julius to be dashing and suave without being creepy. The first time they met, Trevor popped open a special 1998 Riesling wine.

Julius hadn't meant for their meetings to be any different from his usual encounters, and at first they were distinct only by degrees.

As always, he'd arrive at Trevor's place tense. A car service cost at least twenty dollars, so it was harder to justify the expense than when going to Tony's house in the neighborhood. That meant he usually had to schlep through Brooklyn on the train—often even more dressed up in a too-tight, too-well-coordinated outfit than usual, for Trevor's benefit—and to suffer his own constant internal nag the whole way there. How am I walking? Are those people staring at me? Do I look that weird? By the time he'd get to Flatbush he'd be wound into a tight, defensive ball.

He'd walk in and Trevor would offer him a drink. Julius had this part down to a science—accept, but only something light. Trevor would mix himself something classy but potent, a mojito or a gin and tonic, but Julius was always wary of mixing booze with the weed he'd unfailingly been smoking for hours by the time he'd plop down on Trevor's couch. Plus, Trevor would often end up rolling another joint. So Julius kept the drinks to a glass of wine. He'd sip and puff as they'd comfortably rumble through small talk and as Julius slowly warmed to the date.

Which was always helped along by the fact that Trevor and Julius were both temperamentally ill-suited for small talk; they tended to make things bigger, dig into the marrow of a matter rather than pick around the edges. They'd end up talking politics, religion, race—hardly typical pre-hookup banter, but there it was. Idle chat about their backgrounds turned personal, and Trevor explained how he'd moved to the city after growing up in a giant southern family, one of seven kids. He let on about his ambition and drive to set himself apart, to take control of his life and make something out of it. All of that resonated with Julius, and he'd chime in with snips and pieces of the new plan he was busy hatching for his own life, for getting the grand effort of it all back on track before he reached twenty-five. The next thing they knew, what had started off as fifteen minutes of polite conversation before a few hours of sex had flipped on itself; now they'd talk for two and three hours before getting to the bed. "I didn't mind," Julius admits, flashing a defensive smirk.

The sex itself also felt more intimate, even as it shortened.

Julius didn't alter his custom of letting the other party lead on condoms and safety, but Trevor's approach was distinct from many of his other flings. Here, they didn't discuss condoms either, but that's because there was no discussion to be had for Trevor: it was protected sex or no sex. Not that he was a prude. Trevor planned from the start for them to have sprawling, marathon sessions, so he'd always have a row of condoms artfully arranged in a special box by the bed, at the ready. He could get just as freaky as Tony, but the vibe was something else altogether. Julius remembers it wistfully. "Trevor was very different."

Still, Julius didn't drop his guard all the way. He kept control over when and how they met, and studiously avoided inviting Trevor to contact him outside of e-mail or Adam4Adam. He also refused to abandon the passive-aggressive game he played with all his fuck buddies—if Trevor e-mailed, he'd wait hours or even days to respond and set up a meeting, and then often contact him only at the last minute, demanding an immediate audience.

A month into their meetings, Julius walked into Trevor's apartment to find that he'd prepared a romantic dinner for them. It was a brazen step outside of the bounds Julius believed he had set up, but one he couldn't bring himself to reject. For one thing, Trevor could truly cook, something Julius appreciated, being an insatiable cook himself. His housemates would often walk in to find him fixing up a grand meal, something out of place for one person's simple lunch, only to learn he'd been making it for Legba the dog. He appreciated the culinary arts in their own right, and Trevor's skills in them were one more irresistible trait. "He's been a chef with an Italian restaurant—in Italy," Julius explains, waving his hand in the air to signal surrender to the guy's inevitable draw. "Yes, miss honey!" He lights up remembering the night and his face expands into an irrepressible grin. "He's just very sweet."

The meal was seafood, served with more carefully selected

wine. "So good! Soooo good," Julius says, beaming at the memory. "I mean, I won't lie, I liked the attention." He swooned all night as they ate and dove into the usual intensity of their conversations, probing Trevor's effort at "catching the American dream," as Julius puts it, with his slow, steady journey outward from the North Carolina ghetto he grew up in. Julius never said as much to me, but it's hard to imagine he didn't see a bit of what might have been for himself in Trevor. Their goals had been the same: to find freedom and build a life up North through education. Why had it worked out for Trevor, but not Julius? Whatever the reason, Julius's attraction must have been to some degree aspirational. He must have been drawn at least in part to a vision of himself that had long escaped. And maybe that's what made him ultimately flinch at Trevor's determined effort to close the distances Julius had so carefully tended.

Or maybe it was just the baldness of Trevor's break with decorum. Julius usually got there by around 11:00 p.m., and it would be well after four in the morning by the time he trudged back out to the train. That always seemed silly to Trevor, and the evening of the dinner he asked Julius to spend the night.

"No. Obviously, I don't do that," Julius says, recoiling at the memory and asking himself questions he still can't answer. "And after this wonderful dinner he did for me?" His voice drops into a tone one normally reserves for a disappointing experience as he tries to explain what, exactly, Trevor had done to break the spell. "I knew things were going . . ." His voice trails off.

Wherever they were going, Julius decided he wasn't up for the journey. He started cutting Trevor off in the same way he had dismissed Tony: a sudden disappearance, followed by quixotic reappearances when he got lonely or regretful or horny, only to drop away again. "Oh, he's a catch," Julius will acknowledge. "He's got his shit together, a nice guy, da-da, da-da, da-da . . . Me? No."

As frustrating as these conflicting feelings have been to

Julius, Maya Iwata says she saw similar stuff in her work all the time—young people getting their wires crossed on when, where, and how to be vulnerable and intimate. "I'd say, first, that this is hard for everyone," she points out when asked about the travails of sex, dating, and intimacy among the kids she's worked with. "But it's especially hard if the other things that people have in their lives are not there for you." Young folks like Julius develop a set of skills they need to make it through the day, but those skills don't necessarily serve them well in other parts of their lives. "When you are homeless or marginally housed, your survival-based behaviors are cultivated and multiplied," Iwata explains. "It's hard to transition to a space that's something different."

Julius came home pretty shaken up one February night after meeting a john. He came in to Hermone's room to do their usual postwork check-in and took a seat. She asked him what had happened, and as he started to speak he just broke down sobbing. He'd been raped—again.

Hermone had a lot of experience with sexual violence, from her time back at the sex workers' group to her domestic violence interventions and the abortion counseling she'd done. She had to draw on all of that experience to steady herself and be there for Julius that night. He walked her through what happened, and she in turn took him through a spiritual cleansing ritual they'd often done. She bathed him and fixed him up one of her herbal concoctions and generally tried to displace all of the memories of the unwelcome touches with those of a pair of loving, familiar hands. That's all she could do for him. She couldn't make this incident or any of his tumultuous past go away; all she could do is try to displace it in recent memory with what Iwata had called "something different."

Julius would stop tricking after that last rape, at least for the duration of the time that he was in New York City, but his personal sexual life would come completely unhinged. By his accounting, he'd just been through too much with his body and his heart to be responsible for the upkeep of either any longer. "I was dumped. And then three months later I was fucking raped, for the third time," he said to me one day, in an angry and frustrated recounting of his path from the Harlem apartment to the malaise of his East New York life. I had asked him a by then familiar question: What did he think about his rollicking consensual sex life? Why was he taking so many risks that, by his own measure, weren't worth it? "I don't know. After that, I was just like, BOOM." He stopped talking and shook his head as if to chastise himself for even trying to explain this stuff to someone who had no way of really understanding the life he'd led. "I don't wanna talk about it."

A few weeks later, Julius abruptly headed back down to Florida. Hermone is the only one of his New York City friends to have spoken to him since. She holds his travails there in confidence, though when asked about them she will uncharacteristically avert her eyes. Her worries visibly weigh her down.

Julius stood out to Hermone, Lionel, and the others as someone who, despite their efforts to provide breathing space, wasn't making progress while living on Crystal Street. But there were other examples. "When I moved into this house I had very romantic ideas about revolution," Lionel says. "We were gonna build tunnels in the back!" But looking at Julius and some of the people they'd invited into their uprising, he often worried the project had turned into something else. "We went from tunnels to a bunker."

There was no question things had gotten out of hand on Crystal Street: People showed up to hang out with friends and just never left. The spacious front room slowly became a crammed, messy hostel with people sleeping on the floors. As things got overcrowded, squabbling became an issue, petty spats escalated into bigger things. "There was just a lot of drama," says Justin, who never lived there but still felt like he heard constant gripes as the fights and frustrations spilled over into the Village. "I used to visit but then I stopped because I just can't, I can't be sucked into your drama." It was too many people, embroiled in too many quite-real life crises, crammed into too small of a space.

But the rapidity with which the house became overwhelmed was itself a reflection of the deep need it tried to fill, Justin notes. "If someone in the community needed somewhere to go, this is where you could go," he says of the reputation the house developed on the pier. "So it also had that aspect, where people would talk about how it was really good, 'cause it was. It helped a lot of people, people who would have been on the street."

Still, the owners realized, if belatedly, that they were going to have to set up some rules and structures to encourage movement rather than stagnation. Asking everyone who stayed there long-term to come up with $200 a month was part of that effort —and they insisted the money didn't come from any kind of potentially self-destructive activity, at least not that took place inside the house. The rent thing was more of a principled concept than a reality. But there were other, more important rules. For one, you had to actually ask to stay. And the ask-first rule was part of a larger one: if you were gonna live there, you had to have some sort of plan for what you wanted to do next, and how you were going to make it happen. It could be anything—school, a job, reconnecting with family. And there had to be a timeline for putting that plan into action. "I felt like folks were hiding in the house," Hermone explains. "It's kind of like a uterus. Yeah, it's warm and fun, but you've gotta leave. It becomes unhealthy after a while."

But these anxieties aside, the Crystal Street crew couldn't miss noticing, then and now, the cascading impact their efforts at one-on-one healing began to have in East New York. It unfurled dynamically, in much the way Hermone's interaction with the baby dykes had—one brave step fostered the next, which reinforced the last. The friendship between Lionel and Carlos is a perfect example.

Ricky accepted that Carlos wouldn't let him come up from Orlando and visit, but he wouldn't let go of the underlying problem. Carlos needed to come out, he'd lecture. He needed to go tell somebody—anybody—about his sexuality. He'd never be happy otherwise, Ricky warned, never have a real relationship or a real life. Carlos finally listened.

He chose one of his older brothers, Vincent.

Vincent was like all the other men in Carlos's family—macho, tough, streetwise. But he gave a shit too, cared about Carlos and looked out for him. All his brothers always had, really. Things could get dicey in East New York, but in all his years Carlos had never really had any trouble. That was in no small part because Vincent and the others were known to hold their own in a scrape, and because they'd made it known as well that they counted Carlos's welfare among the things they stood ready to fight about.

And Vincent was also one of those Carlos had boasted to about the supposed girlfriend from Florida that he'd met online, going on and on about how beautiful and smart she was. So he figured that gave him a viable entrée into the conversation. He cornered Vincent and awkwardly backed into the point.

"I have to talk to you," he began, horrified at the words he planned to speak next. "You know that girl I talk to? It's really a guy." He spelled out that he was trying to say he was gay—and then he started crying.

But as is too often the case, all Vincent had needed to embrace Carlos's sexuality was to be given a chance to do so. In fact, as Vincent pointed out, the boys had a gay uncle. He had been among the hordes of gay New Yorkers slain in the late 1980s by

AIDS, so Carlos wasn't old enough to have understood what was going on with him as a child. But Vincent had grown up with the man. He'd taken Vincent around the city, showed him his Manhattan neighborhood, and deliberately exposed him to all kinds of things beyond East New York, things that Carlos and his other siblings would never get a chance to experience growing up. Vincent remembered their uncle reverently.

"You know, I loved your uncle," Vincent told him. "I was great with your uncle, so I'm OK with you being gay too."

Today, Carlos talks mournfully about the missed opportunities his uncle's premature death set up. The part of his relationship with his uncle that he remembers most vividly and tangibly is watching as AIDS strangled away his life. His lover died first, and soon thereafter the virus began ravaging his own body. Carlos describes the spectacle succinctly: "It was terrible." He watched as his mom stood by her brother. And he watched as others in the family grew cagey, as they began avoiding him and warning their children not to touch the coffee mugs he drank from, lest they catch the disease, too. "But it was ignorance," Carlos says with understanding. "The whole thing was just starting."

He paints fantastic pictures in his mind of the life his uncle must have lived, ensconced in his Chelsea apartment and overflowing with the freedom and success he associates with a gay world he's never touched himself. "As a child, I had no idea, but his lover was always around us," Carlos will explain, adding boastfully, "He had that extravagant gay life—the college thing, and a great job in the hospital." And even with the short time he has spent cobbling together his own gay life since coming out to Vincent, when remembering his uncle's death Carlos is already able to connect the dots. He's all too aware of the impact the AIDS epidemic has had on his development: in slaughtering a generation of gay men like his uncle—men whose ranks were and still are disproportionately filled with people of color—the virus has hamstrung young gay men in the already difficult process of finding someone to help them make the calculated-risk choices that Robert Garofalo and Maya Iwata talk about. Sitting in the apartment he shares with his parents today, twenty-five years old and not long out of the closet, still struggling to find a version of gay community that he can relate to and still trying to shed the emotional scales accumulated during an adolescence spent in deep denial, Carlos thinks about his dead gay uncle and sums up his regret better than any social scientist could. "If he would have stayed alive," he says, "he could have helped me with being gay so much."

Carlos and Lionel both grew up alongside AIDS. Carlos has never been alive without the epidemic, which officially started in 1981, and Lionel, in his early thirties in 2007, has certainly never been sexually active without it. So if gay life can be divided into pre- and post-AIDS, those who knew something of a world without it and those who don't, Lionel can't offer Carlos much in the way of mentorship. Indeed, in Lionel's eyes they're basically peers, both trying to figure out late in life how to honestly and healthily incorporate their sexuality into their lives. Like Carlos, Lionel comes from a traditional family rooted in an immigrant-identified culture; his is simply Asian rather than Latin. The details are different but the rules of communal and familial belonging feel the same—don't edge out of the closet too fast, don't jeopardize a sure support system for vague and uncertain notions of joining a gay world that looks particularly white from the outside. If anything, Lionel was just a few steps ahead of Carlos in this process, propelled along by distance from his family and by the swirling hyperqueer environment his ex-girlfriend had thrust him into. Still, those few steps were something, a small resource where there weren't many others to be found, so Carlos's brother Vincent considered it a big score when he found out about Lionel.

At the time Lionel began inching out of the closet, he and Vincent were spending a lot of time together. As part of Lionel's housing organizing work, the two of them were trying to get the tenants of Vincent's apartment building together to clean up the place and take ownership of it from the city.

After the fire that chased Vincent and Carlos's family out of their building years previously, a number of the residents made their way back to the block. When Carlos and his folks left the Red Cross shelter, they found their way back to East New York through Section 8 housing, and eventually even moved back to their old block as well. But Vincent and his wife had been among those who were, in strictly legal terms, squatting in the partially damaged building next door to the one they'd been burned out of. It offered a makeshift home at best for most of its tenants. The electricity didn't work right, nor did the water. Drug dealers had taken over large swaths of the building and set up shop. And the city had recently claimed it, and was plotting its own redevelopment plan. Lionel and Vincent wanted the process to be driven by the erstwhile tenants rather than the city, and they'd hunkered down together to rally Vincent's neighbors for the long slog forward to tenant ownership.

The campaign was a pressure cooker, and one way they'd blow off steam was by taking long bike rides through Brooklyn. They'd wend their way through the borough's sprawling central corridor and share little pieces of themselves along the route. During one of these rides, they had stopped at a random pizza joint underneath a stretch of the Brooklyn-Queens Expressway when Lionel turned to Vincent and told him he was gay.

"I remember being really scared. I don't know why," Lionel says. But he pressed on anyway. "I needed to tell somebody."

He had no reason to fear. Vincent was glad to hear it, because he'd been worried about Carlos. The kid needed a role model, he must've been thinking, somebody to help him avoid whatever mistakes had killed his uncle. A couple of days later he tracked Lionel down. "I want you to talk to my brother," he said. "He's going through things. He's gay, but he doesn't know what to do. There's questions and stuff like that."

Lionel may have been an unlikely gay mentor for Carlos, but he rose to the job, aided by the fact that, by this point, he had a house full of queer kids to help him out. The place had become all gay, all the time. "It was loud," Hermone jokes about how the house suddenly changed when queerness took over. "People voguing in the living room, and just talking about the issues. It was just all very gay." And Lionel figured the best way to help Carlos was to bring him around all that gayness.

After Vincent introduced the two, Lionel had been open and outgoing as usual. He'd invite Carlos to movies, urge him to come by the house. But Carlos was reluctant. Not just because he was nervous, which he certainly was, but also because as soon as he met Lionel he got a crush. That was partly out of the novelty of interacting with another gay man—"he was like the first gay guy..." Carlos giggles in embarrassment at the memory—and partly because Lionel is an undoubtedly handsome and charming figure. In any case, Carlos was as always distrustful of himself and his ability to betray feelings he'd rather keep hidden. "I didn't want him to think I was flaky," Carlos explains. "So I kind of avoided him, 'cause I didn't want to like push up on him or anything like that. But I think he knew."

Lionel was actually oblivious, distracted by his own newness to the situation. And he had a different match in mind for Carlos: he really wanted him to meet Manny, who had joined the FIERCE! members' migration to East New York and moved into the house. Manny had come a long way to arrive on Crystal Street, and by this point considered himself a seasoned gay veteran. And by any measure, he was. He'd managed to not just take care of himself on his own, but in many instances to thrive.

After storming out on Cassandra, he spent a month in his

coworkers' guestroom before he wore out his welcome. During that month, he cut off complete contact with his mom, insistently ignoring her calls to his cell phone and refusing to contact her himself. As she thrashed about looking for him, she'd found David's home contact information and spoken to his parents—outing the guy to them in the process of searching for Manny and sparking a fight that sent David storming from his family's Queens home, too. That's part of why Manny had to leave his coworkers' house. Supporting one wayward gay kid was one thing, but housing him and his boyfriend was too much for them.

So Manny and David worked their wide network of white politicos—mostly in the then-waning East Village radical arts and activism scene—and couch-surfed from one temporary home to another for the next couple of years. Most of that time was spent in the small Greenwich Village loft of an older, white gay man who was something of a celebrity in the downtown gay arts world. "When I first met him, I was like, does he wanna fuck me?" Manny says of the man. "But it wasn't that at all." It turned out the guy wanted nothing more than to keep Manny and David off the streets, and in that regard he offered the sort of no-strings adult support that homeless gay kids too rarely get.

Manny looks upon those days fondly. He had a boyfriend he loved, a roof over his head, and he was at the center of just the sort of outsider political and social scene he'd always envisioned himself to be cut out for. He and David were celebrities in their own right, a pair of precocious, colored gay teens who could mix and mingle with their white elders with ease. They hung out at the famed Bowery Poetry Club. They helped the guy they lived with throw a weekly film party that was *the* place to be if you considered yourself a hip, downtown queer artist. And, eventually, Manny even found FIERCE!

He wouldn't let on about it, but finding FIERCE! had been a big coup. Here was a place where he could finally be all of himself—not just a radical queer, not just a black kid from Brooklyn, but both. It took him some time to let his guard down there. He still didn't have much in common with most of the membership—the kids like Justin whose lives literally revolved around the pier. And he'd never given up that instinct for preemptive strike when he felt out of place. So, as usual, he wielded his otherness as a sign of superiority, an exotic experience others in the space couldn't understand. There was, for instance, the fact that he'd already spent two years involved in high-profile antiwar activism, ever since he'd dropped out of school. He wouldn't let others in the group forget that resume.

"He had an attitude, and I didn't appreciate it," says Justin, voicing a common read on Manny, at least among members, if not with staff like Hermone. "There were things he did know better than me. But you don't keep putting that out—keep, keep putting that out. That's not cute." Still, like others, Justin had to acknowledge that Manny did in fact have the benefit of a unique set of experiences—though few knew the full story of the life in which he'd honed what, for him, were simply survival skills—and that it gave him something most in the scene desperately longed for themselves: confidence. "If you got that confidence, then..." Justin trails off, not actually sure what it would have meant to have such a thing at that age. "I never had that confidence."

Lionel picked up on Manny's steady self-assurance too, and he thought that's just what Carlos needed a shot of. So he wanted the pair to meet. He invited Carlos to a barbecue that Hermone and all the queer roommates threw in the garden one afternoon, and stayed after him to actually show up.

Ricky had long ago gotten sick of waiting around for Carlos to come out and had broken things off, leaving Carlos once again isolated. His cajoling had helped push Carlos into telling Vincent, who spread the news to the rest of the family, but Carlos still hadn't gone beyond that in being out in the neighborhood. So attending the barbecue was a bold, public move. He knew he'd be seen in the mix of all those identifiably queer folks, and that scared him. "This area, when I was young, if you saw one gay person it was a big deal. And that person was that flamboyant, loud-mouth gay that everyone basically laughed at." He didn't want to be seen as that caricature, but nor did he want to keep living the way he was living. Beyond Lionel, the only outlet he had for interacting with other gay people was the Internet, and even that had gone sour since Ricky dumped him. "I was heartbroken because of that," he regretfully admits. "I loved him." He needed more in his life, and Lionel was offering it. So he went.

It helped that it was a pretty Brooklyn afternoon, and scared though he may have been, Carlos was feeling the summer vibe. It also helped when he looked up to see Manny offering him a plate of food. If he'd been wobbly-kneed about Lionel, Manny knocked him flat out. "I looked and I was like, wow! I like him. I have this thing: I love black men. I *love* them." And Manny had blackness down by now—his light mustache over his smooth, dark brown skin; close-cropped hair and a thick, stout build; a slow, suave cadence that deftly mixed brainy verbiage with Brooklyn-boy street lingo. Carlos was plain turned on and had no idea how to handle it. He went with a schoolboy's instinct for acting like you don't want what you most desire. "I was like, 'I'm not hungry.' I was probably playing hard to get!" He laughs, not clear himself on what he thought he was accomplishing—particularly since Manny wasn't really chasing; he'd only approached Carlos in the first place because Lionel asked him to.

They exchanged little glances and flirts throughout the afternoon, but both of them were more preoccupied with the giddy novelty of the event itself. Here they were, in the middle of a tiny green oasis inside a neighborhood best known for the things that have been destroyed there—properties, families, communities, lives—building an entirely new black and brown queer space, literally planting a rainbow flag in the ground. "I thought, wow, this house is right *here?*" Carlos remembers feeling at the picnic. "It made me feel really comfortable and I was —I was happy to be gay."

ELEVEN

Manny, Julius, Lionel, and all the rest of them over on Crystal Street are driving Carlos crazy today. It's already late afternoon, and the day's almost wasted. He's been all dressed up and ready to go, pacing around his apartment like this since early morning. He knows they've certainly missed the parade by now. He'll have to wait till next year to stand along Eighth Avenue and cheer as the drag queens and marching bands and floats packed with half-naked guys in body paint and sequins frolic through the city. Now he's just hoping they'll get down to Christopher while the street festival is still going on. It's his first time going to gay pride, after all. Don't they get that? For that matter, he's not been down to the piers for any purpose more than just a handful of times.

Young Keith was cool enough to take him down to the Village and Christopher Street earlier this summer. After their days tossing uncertain and suspicious looks at one another on the block, Keith and Carlos finally connected as reps from the neighborhood itself in the gay hubbub of Hermone and Lionel's house—which itself seemed to both of them to be an unbelievable place, like some sort of all-gay version of MTV's *Real World* right there in East New York. Carlos had felt a little strange being shown around the Village by someone so much younger than he, but so it goes. Keith had had the dubious advantage of being too flaming to hide it, and thus had been able to start exploring gay life before Carlos. He gets that he's come to the party late, and he's really just eager to start making up for lost time.

Today, though, he's also nervous, so he's trying not to be too much of a spaz by blowing up Lionel's phone with too many calls. He's anxious about being around that many gay people in the city—not because he's fearful, but because he's champing at the bit to finally be out in the open and in the majority. He's gotten used to stalking around the neighborhood as a gay man, even if he—like Lionel—feels as if most people don't really know about him. But Manhattan and the Village, that's the big leagues. He's finally going to get a real taste of what everybody else at the house is always talking about. And his stomach butterflies aren't just about gay pride, either. There's also Manny. He's really hoping they'll get a chance to spend some time talking today. Manny seemed interested at the barbecue, Carlos thinks, but he fears he played it too coy and gave the wrong impression. He wants another chance at it.

Manny, like most of the other queers living on Crystal, couldn't care less about pride. They've been enough times to consider it dull, and to them the jam-packed crowd sounds more off-putting than alluring. That's why it's taking so long; many of the others aren't particularly interested in going, Lionel and his new boyfriend included, who are the ones leading the expedition in Lionel's van.

Manny's also not particularly interested in Carlos. Lionel had pulled him aside at the barbecue and told him there was somebody he should meet, but Manny hadn't took it like *that*—that Carlos was some fresh-out-of-the-closet queen in search of first love and who needed to be treated with kid gloves. Carlos was cute, Manny thought, and he could see hooking up with him, but that was about it. Nevertheless, Manny can already see the guy has stars in his eyes, so he'll have to keep him at arm's length today, until he can sort out how to handle it. The whole affair seems like sort of a hassle. But this is how it goes with family holidays—and Manny knows that's what today is, no matter how corny the concept. It's their big day, and Lionel's been playing dad-*cum*-community-organizer all week in rallying every queer he can muster in the neighborhood to come along. There are worse things, Manny thinks, and he'll do his part to show Carlos and the other newbies a good time, because he considers himself as much of a leader in this social realm of East New York as he does in the politics of FIERCE! and the West Village. And he is.

As things had heated up back in the summer of 2002, Manny had in fact brought to the pier campaign invaluable hands-on experience from dealing with media in the high-stakes, pressurized moments of the antiwar movement. That spring, a coalition of residents' groups staged a rally in Sheridan Square—onetime home to the street kids of Stonewall—to rev up support for intensified policing in the coming summer. FIERCE! held a counterrally that outnumbered them; and Manny worked with the media team to steal the attention of the press the residents had arranged to cover their event. They even managed to keep out of the press an incident they all loved but thought might not be the best PR: a number of pier kids stormed the front of the residents' press conference and began chanting, in mocking irony of what they held to be the residents' true concerns, "Give us your money! Give us your homes!"

By the time of that press conference, the problem had so intensified not just because of the politics, but because of the logistics. The state had closed down the West Side piers completely by then, in order to finish its grand waterfront-redevelopment plan, which was designed at least in part to stoke the area's already raging real estate market. That meant that the hundreds of kids who had hung out on the Christopher Street pier every night had no place else to go but the surrounding streets. "I just showed up one day and the pier was fenced off,"

Justin says, describing how abruptly the whole thing happened. "I'd just been there the night before." He knew about the construction, of course, but he hadn't seen or heard anything about the piers being totally closed off. "I took it as my life being threatened," he calmly explains, using language he in no way considers hyperbole. Hundreds of others agreed, and that's when the FIERCE! meetings started overflowing. They'd schedule an organizational planning meeting and dozens of people would turn up. Shocked and overwhelmed, they'd just turn the planning meetings into organizer trainings. The energy built upon itself, Justin explains, as the now doubly rootless young people started buzzing about the campaign. The mood was angry, but also optimistic—"We're gonna do this," he remembers people saying and feeling. "We're gonna get our pier back."

Bob Kohler fears that optimism, while essential, was and remains misplaced, because the problem now is bigger than simple NIMBY politics. "I don't know who is going to give up the space, because any space in the Village is worth millions of dollars," he admits. Kohler and his gay-liberation politics are as much of a relic in today's West Village as the antiques that fill the apartment he's lived in for decades. "This particular apartment and this street, if I had told somebody I lived on Charles Street they would never have known where it was. It was just a street, with just—apartments, that's all. Nothing special. Now? Hilary Swank lived next door. Sarah Jessica Parker down the street. Gwyneth Paltrow was around the corner. You just get—it's crazy." With homes selling for as much as $10 million—and no less than $2 or $3 million—even longtime residents realized things were going to have to change in the neighborhood—on Christopher, on those broken-down old piers, and with the kids that populated both. "The money spoiled everything. And rich people smell the money coming before everybody else. You know, they're on the inside track there. So they know what's coming. And they said, 'Well, we can't have this.'"

To be fair, particularly once the piers closed down, the noise and crowds and general fuss in the West Village's once relatively peaceful streets was undeniable. Unable to hang out on the pier, the kids hung out on people's stoops and along the sidewalks. Everything that once went on out of sight and out of mind—sequestered across the four-lane highway of West Street and hanging off the edge of the island—now took place cheek by jowl with condo owners and boutique store managers and celebrity home-buyers. And Justin's twelve-hour rotations in the area were hardly unique; people hang out making noise all night long. Not to mention that for the scores of young people who have nowhere to go home to each night, the Village is considered the safest place to pass the city's midnight hours. All of which generates understandable gripes from the area's propertied residents. "Just because they're rich doesn't mean they don't deserve a night's sleep," Kohler scolds. "And simply because you sleep all day, that doesn't mean that anybody else can. So that's always been something I've said to the kids. I will not support you screaming all night long up and down the streets. And not *everybody* is rich."

As the battle has raged on, this is one point on which FIERCE! and the neighborhood groups have been able to hammer out something of a détente. FIERCE! has held off efforts to push back the curfew on the remodeled pier, holding the line at one in the morning, and in return has agreed to help build a culture of self-policing among the young people, encouraging them to be as respectful as possible of their propertied neighbors. But what the organizers have been unable to achieve is getting more money to build safe spaces like the Neutral Zone back in the area, offering meaningful alternatives to the streets. And that, says Kohler, is the fight they're unlikely to win—because ultimately the neighborhood wants them to be gone altogether. "They're a liability," he bluntly concludes, and they're fighting for a space that really no longer exists. "But that doesn't mean they shouldn't fight for it."

That's the message Justin and Manny and their friends gathered to give the neighborhood in October 2002, after months of push and pull with the resident groups and cops and politicians in meetings that dragged on all summer. They dubbed it a festival rather than a protest or a rally, and advertised it with posters all over the neighborhood, succinctly calling on queer youth to "Reclaim Our Space."

The event started with a press conference Manny and the media task force organized in Sheridan Square. They'd set up a stage at the front edge of the small park, facing out onto Seventh Avenue and staring down the mouth of Christopher Street. A group of youth and allies stood in a semicircle on the stage, behind a lone microphone at which one speaker after another talked about the importance of the space they were there to reclaim. The goal was to reframe the issue from a simple battle over the residents' quality of life versus the kids' right to run the streets. The point, FIERCE! maintained, was that aggressive policing would solve no one's problems: poor queer teens of color would still have nowhere else to go, and for each batch the cops dragged off to detention centers another would ultimately flow in to replace them. What was needed was more, not less, services for the youth in the Village—and primarily the same thing they'd been looking for since Stonewall, a place for them to not just go to but belong in.

Justin's job was to help bring it all home more emotively by reading a poem he'd written, about his years growing up on the pier with his boyfriend Jamal and his friends. But as he stood behind the stage, he panicked; he couldn't muster that confidence thing he'd chafed at in Manny. He couldn't stop imagining himself tripping on the single, foot-high box-step he'd have to climb to get to the microphone, where he'd then have to stand unshielded in front of this massive crowd. Everybody else seemed able to talk off the top of their head, or have memorized what they were going to say, and that made him more nervous. He had his poem written out on two loose-leaf pieces of paper and would surely have to read every word of it. He had every intention of backing out. In the end, he only went through with it because his best friend somehow convinced him that she'd never talk to him again if he didn't.

When Justin's turn came he climbed onto the stage—managing not to trip, after all—and walked up to the mike. He looked down at his paper and started to read, and as he'd feared he couldn't get the words out right. He stumbled and stuttered through the first two lines and then stopped. This was more than he could do, more than he'd ever been asked to do. He had helped make a documentary about the piers the previous fall, before the acrimonious fight with the neighbors really heated up. But in that he was a behind-the-scenes producer; he had steadfastly refused to be seen on camera. Now, here he was on this stage with all these people staring at him, reporters included, barely able to hang on to his own thoughts and emotions written out on these pieces of paper. He wanted out, and yet he knew it was too late for that. "I just closed my eyes and took a breath and was like, 'OK, let me start again.'" This time he kept his head down and plowed through to the end, speaking clearly enough to be understood, he hoped. It wasn't until he heard the applause at the end that he realized he'd accomplished something remarkable, that he'd stood up and told the world that he belonged here just like anybody else, and try though they may, they weren't going to sweep him away. "I was like, well, you should have clapped at the beginning!" he jokes now, flashing his broad grin. "Then I would have been OK."

Having stood up, Justin couldn't sit back down. After the press conference, the throngs of youth and their allies lined up and marched down Christopher toward the pier, and Justin made his way to the front to be among the leaders. They had erected a small stage at the corner of Christopher and West Streets, in front of what was then a porn video store. And once they arrived there, rather than rail and chant the kids performed. For three hours, they read spoken word, they sang, they vogued. This sort of creativity would become a staple of FIERCE!'s organizing efforts. When a group of Religious Right activists came to New York City to protest government money supporting the Harvey Milk School for gay kids, FIERCE! transformed the first day of school into a fashion runway event, cheering students as they arrived and showering them with glitter, all while creating a human shield blocking out the protesters. A later public space demonstration would be built around a ball. They chose to use the talents and skills they possessed to make organic statements rather than trying to cram their voices into staid forms that would poorly articulate their goals anyway. As one organizer reportedly told cops who eventually ordered the October festival to end—because FIERCE! had a permit for a protest and was instead throwing a block party—"This is how gay people protest."

When the East New York gaggle finally climbs out of Lionel's van and into the city's gay pride crowd, Carlos is blown away. The bodies are crammed together like sardines, stretching through the streets as far as the eye can see. And as they wind through the confusing maze of police barricades and slowly pick their way westward toward the waterfront and the Christopher Street pier, the tanned flesh of shirtless white men becomes increasingly rare as black and brown bodies begin to dominate the landscape. As the mash of flesh changes so does the police presence and posture. The cops' crowd-control tactics grow more aggressive, their tone sharpens as they order people to and fro. The metal, mobile fences they've erected at intersections funnel foot traffic through increasingly narrowed spaces.

Street traffic throughout downtown Manhattan has been redirected all day to accommodate the tens of thousands of gay revelers that take over the city every year on this day, but down here by the piers it is the black and brown festival goers who are diverted to accommodate traffic. Streets up and down the Village's western edge dump out onto the highway that runs alongside the newly remodeled and landscaped waterfront, but cops are allowing passage through only one spot, at Christopher, which itself cannot be approached from just any of the half-dozen intersecting streets but must be entered at its mouth several blocks back. All of this turns the simple process of getting onto and off of the piers into a tense, hours-long affair in and of itself.

Once there, every inch of available space is filled with young black and Latino queers, and most of the East New York crew can't be bothered with it all. They've each seen better days down here on the piers, without the pretty landscaping and without the cranky cops tasked with protecting it. That means that after a day of waiting around to get down here, they're all ready to go back pretty quickly. Carlos is frustrated with the truncated time frame, but again, he knows he's come late to all this gay stuff. He'll have to make up the time on his own somehow. So he tries to just enjoy the time he's got at the festival, and the fireworks alone are worth the trip.

He also notices how Keith comes alive down here, too. He'd watched the kid go through the same sort of transformation on their previous trips to Christopher Street—and this time he's stripped off the loose-fitting clothes he'd been wearing back in East New York to reveal a tighter-fitting purple shirt that he's cut slices into, letting his dark, black skin peek out through the pattern. "It's his time to shine, too," Carlos laughs to himself.

Manny notices Keith's opening up as well. They've been hanging out together a lot back on Crystal Street. They don't have all that much in common, really, but Manny's drawn to a memory of his former fourteen-year-old self when watching and talking with Keith. It's like the first time the kid had sex, and came running over to the house to tell Manny about it. As Manny listened he had imagined what it would have been like for him had there been a house like theirs on Eastern Parkway, someplace where he could have flopped down on a nineteen-year-old black gay boy's bed and gushed about his initial experimenting with Jason, rather than being left to depend on the willing but entirely unfamiliar sounding board of his white girlfriend Lisa. What would that have looked like for him? He can't imagine. But he likes the idea of Keith living out this bizarre, alternate reality, so he encourages the kid to come around.

They've made their way back off the piers and are walking along in the Village when Keith freaks out. He sees one of his teachers and thinks to hide, but it's too late and the man spots him.

"What are you doing down here?" he asks, shocked to see the boy. "Does your mom know you're here?"

Keith shrinks, and Carlos thinks he suddenly looks embarrassed by his outfit. Keith explains to the guy that he's here with his neighbors, and the man—who Carlos doesn't think looks terribly comfortable in the encounter, either—accepts that answer and disappears into the crowd. Soon thereafter, Keith's back to his former bubbling self, and Carlos is glad to see Keith has the strength to shrug it off and not let it ruin his day.

And Keith had in fact moved on, but not just on the strength of his own singular will. Manny had actually pulled him aside and turned the uncomfortable encounter into a joke on the teacher, rather than on Keith. Look, he'd said, even your teacher's a fag. They'd laughed, and it had boosted Keith's spirits back up, made him see the run-in as the small, insignificant event that it was. Manny gave him perspective on things like that, gave him a lens through which to view the tumult of adolescence he was wading into.

ACKNOWLEDGMENTS

This book is made possible first and foremost by the fact that the young people who are profiled here were willing to share with me not just dozens of hours of their time, but also many of their deepest vulnerabilities. It took incredible acts of trust to open themselves to me in the way that they did. And in many cases they broached subjects and memories they had not previously examined even privately, let alone for the purpose of journalism. They gained nothing for this sacrifice, but did so in the belief that by sharing their own struggles and victories they could help others facing the same challenges. This bravery was but one of the many ways in which each of the people I have written about proved to me just how remarkable they are. I am deeply indebted to them, and I believe our communities are as well.

I am also indebted to my editor Brian Halley and his colleagues at Beacon Press. Beacon was an enthusiastic backer of this project from its inception, immediately grasping the import of a story that is too easily dismissed as marginal. Brian skillfully and patiently guided me along in trying to live up to the great responsibility of compelling and accurately telling that important story. It is conventional wisdom that nonfiction book authors can expect little of their editors in today's publishing marketplace. I am gratefully ignorant of such an experience. I enjoyed an engaged, inquisitive, and dedicated editor in Brian, and without that resource this book would not have been completed.

Thanks also to Colin, Gary, and the crew at Outpost Café for being spectacular hosts for me and the neighborhood's other office-shy workers. A special thanks goes out to my friend and colleague Kenyon Farrow, whose grassroots journalism and activism famously places him at the epicenter of all things queer and colored in New York City. He's the first person I turned to in looking for sources for this story, and his contacts made the book possible. But the list of loved ones in my life who enable all of my work is far too long to detail. From family to friends to co-conspirators, I have always been blessed by a support system that is both wide and deep. They are understanding when I neglect them during chaotic deadline crunches, and they are embracing when I reemerge in manic search of stress relief. Most of all, they provide the unconditional love that we all long for and that I, for one, desperately need, not only to survive but to flourish. Thank you all.

Printed in the United States
by Baker & Taylor Publisher Services